Second Nature

ANDREI NAVROZOV

Second Nature

FORTY-SIX POEMS

BY

BORIS PASTERNAK

PETER OWEN
London and Chester Springs

ISBN 0 7206 1192 X

Extracts from T.S Eliot's 'The Metaphysical Poets'
in *Selected Essays* (originally published in 1921)
are reprinted by permission of Faber and Faber Limited.

PETER OWEN PUBLISHERS
73 Kenway Road, London SW5 0RE

First published in Great Britain 1990
This paperback edition published 2003
Introduction, notes and this translation
© Andrei Navrozov 1990

Printed and bound in Great Britain by
Bookmarque Ltd, Croydon, Surrey

Contents

INTRODUCTION

Transporting the Elements

To the memory of Alexander Bisk
'Sein Bild: ich weih's.' (Rilke)

A visitor to modern Athens, if he is inclined to contemplation, will be startled by a Greek word emblazoned on lorries, vans, and often on tiny estate cars, whose owners make a living by hauling the cargoes of industry and the belongings of men from place to place as they have done since the beginning of history. The word is *Metaphorai*. It is less likely that a Greek-speaking resident of the city should be quite as affected by the presence of an idea so profound in surroundings so mundane. Nor is it any easier to imagine an English-speaking denizen of New York dumbstruck at the sight of the word *Transport* on the side of a moving truck, even if he became convinced that inside it were priceless artefacts bound for Sotheby's sale-rooms.

My aim, in offering these versions of Pasternak's poems, is to bring the Russian poet to the English-speaking world. Reduced to its Latin roots, 'translation' mirrors the Greek for 'metaphor', and the original working title of this collection, which I began working on some twelve years ago, was 'Transport of Elements'. The elements I had in mind were Pasternak's, but also, in their broader and deeper meaning, those of Russian verse, for only an iota of sense separates *stikhi*, derived from the Greek word for their orderly stance, and the great elemental *stikhii* of Aristotle. With the passing of years, the present title has evolved, capturing I believe the essential simplicity inherent in the work of a translator. I shall return to this subject later, addressing for the time being the essential difficulties of the task, present side by side with that simplicity.

When Horace transposed Aeolian song to the everlasting 'Italian mode', when Chopin transcribed simple village tunes in his polonaises and mazurkas, the spiritual cargo they were transporting can be said to have consisted of raw material. My cargo, by contrast, consists of a single meticulously crafted, priceless and unique cultural object which, if it is to be understood and appreciated by its recipients, must arrive whole, in one piece, ideally with the supporting stylobate of its cultural history still intact. This last is called a biography, and a suitable life of Pasternak remains to be written.

The literary reputation of Boris Pasternak in the West resembles a novel based on the life of an imaginary artist, a hypothetical figure along the lines of Adrian Leverkühn, the composer hero of Thomas Mann's *Doctor Faustus*. However much the English reader learns about the man, his work, like Leverkühn's music, remains a mystery. To be sure, the work is discussed, criticized, explained. Yet it does not exist. Is this, to use a phrase beloved of our critics, a problem of translation? I would rather present it as a problem of life or love – which, to a Christian or a poet, are the only elements worth thinking about in the first place.

I should like to begin with a truism, uttered with the confidence of St Paul's familiar words to the Corinthians which echo in Whitsuntide through the churches of Cambridge outside my window. A poet should never describe what he cannot love. Let us regard this breezy truism as a most solemn truth. Indeed, whatever the semantic implications of 'transport', it must be agreed at the outset that its emotional connotations are nothing if not sincere.

There are forty-six poems in this book. Not fifty, or a round hundred. Not *The Complete Poems of Boris Pasternak*, not *The Complete Early Poems*, nor even *Complete Poems: 1912–1932*. As she looked, in 1933, at what was then – and unbeknown to her would remain – the poet's final harvest, Marina Tsvetayeva exclaimed with prescient finality: 'Half a thousand pages'.

From these, I have chosen a mere handful. But in life as in love, is there really such a thing as choice?

When I was a child, I knew those five hundred pages by heart. The task of selection was neither frustrating nor gratifying, since T. S. Eliot's 'question of some nicety' to 'decide how much must be read of any particular poet' was never meant for children. When I became a man, I knew I had to do only what I could, and as much of it as I could.

The infatuation of a nine-year-old resolved an even more important problem of translation. As a child, I found in Pasternak a beauty which lay in something other than the 'meaning' of his poems. I use the word in its most unsophisticated sense: I simply did not understand many of the words. It was only later that I discovered a contemporary critic, Nikolai Aseev, who wrote that in his friend's verse 'the element of intonation predominates and is the *raison d'être* of the whole poem'. I do not think this is true today, and neither did Pasternak, but I certainly would have agreed with Aseev intuitively at the age of nine. When my vocabulary matured, encompassing the full 'meaning' of Pasternak's verse, my original, child's feeling did not shrink. The content of love filled the form and became an object.

In an article on translation, R. A. Brower has written:

We translate the less familiar by putting the more familiar in its place, and when the right occasion comes along, we are prepared to use the once forgotten gesture or word 'like a native'. Much of our learning of our own language takes place through similar processes. The child points to a farmer in a hayfield and says – as I once heard a child say – 'Man haying' and the parent, who speaks the foreign language of the adult world, *dutifully corrects and translates*, 'The man is haying'. [My italics – A.N.]

Applied to Pasternak, in this case, such a learning process would entail the perpetual translation of his poetry into Russian, which is precisely what my love of him as a child has prevented me from doing as a man. Conceived *in puris naturalibus*, this love never needed correction and remains blind to duty.

I am not exaggerating the temptation to translate Pasternak into Russian. It is great, and few resist it completely. Still fewer are those who have resisted it for reasons other than ordinary contempt, intellectual idleness, or spiritual inadequacy, all of which a poet encounters in his critics. Here is one contemporary, discussing, in 1928, Pasternak's 'limitations':

> If we add to them a deficiency of taste – which was innate in him, though maybe later it became a matter of principle – we shall understand why he has had to go through a long struggle to free the language of his verse from various kinds of weeds all equally evident in it: near-meaningless un-Russian turns of speech, dubious stresses, incorrect cases and wrongly abbreviated endings. [Examples from *My Sister Life* and *Themes & Variations* follow – A.N.] This outrageous example is characteristic because it shows not only a lack of taste but also a deficiency of thought, that is, insufficient realization of how words should be used; and this is something from which Pasternak will never quite escape, nor can any more lately acquired knowledge of the language cure him of it. Indeed, such knowledge will always remain somewhat inert, pointless, founded more on a reading of dictionaries than on a deepening of linguistic awareness.

The author, a Russian émigré named Wladimir Weidle, became, thirty years later, a verbose admirer of 'mature' Pasternak and did not take the opportunity to revise his view of the 'early' work in his introduction to the most complete collection of the poet's writings published outside of Russia. How the Weidles of the world become the executors of spiritual estates which its Pasternaks leave behind is a mystery not unique to the Russian emigration, but I had better reflect on that elsewhere.

Vicious or ecstatic, contemporary Russian critics agree that the poetic world of Pasternak is as autonomous as it is unique: although created in language, it is outside language. Khlebnikov once called him 'the youthful German of Russian speech', and to Tsvetayeva's ears his speech was at once the gurgling of a baby ('and this baby is the world') and the wordless joy of an even younger earth ('created *before* Adam'): 'Pasternak doesn't speak, hasn't time to finish speaking.' But Khlebnikov and Tsvetayeva were themselves poets of genius, and their impressions are not representative. We need to turn to the best of the average, a critic or two with nothing more than a good ear between them. They concur. In 1922 Ilya Ehrenburg wrote:

> It's hard work talking to Pasternak. His speech is a combination of tongue-twisting, a desperate straining to drag out a needed word from within, and a stormy cascade of unexpected comparisons, complex associations and frank confessions in what is evidently a foreign language. He would be unintelligible were not all this chaos illumined by the singleness and clarity of his voice.

In 1924 Yuri Tynyanov quoted the penultimate stanza of 'Poetry' (p. 59), concluding much to the same effect: 'This is almost an instance of "meaningless soundspeech", and yet it is inexorably logical; it is a kind of phantom imitation of syntax, and yet the syntax here is impeccable.' Another critic, writing in 1927, summed up: 'Pasternak writes unintelligibly because he wants to write unintelligibly.'

This, then, is the difference between Pasternak and the child in the hayfield. The child of three one may 'correct and translate' into the language that is his by education. To do this to a poet of twenty-three, in a language that is so utterly his by birth, is to make a mockery of the breezy truism whose acceptance as a most solemn truth I require of myself and my reader.

'Like the original poet,' wrote Renato Poggioli, 'the translator is a Narcissus who chooses to contemplate his own likeness not in the spring of nature but in the pool of art.' Let us try to recapture that moment of contemplation. Obviously, among the first things to come to mind is the question of what its end result would be like. Where would the world of Pasternak 'fit' in the universe of English prosody? Turn to Pasternak's 'Definition of Poetry' (p. 28). Is there room for his star in our pond?

Here is T. S. Eliot, Pasternak's contemporary, writing in 1921:

> The poets of the seventeenth century, the successors of the dramatists of the sixteenth, possessed a mechanism of sensibility which could devour any kind of experience. . . . In the seventeenth century a dissociation of sensibility set in, from which we have never recovered; and this dissociation, as is natural, was aggravated by the influence of the two most powerful poets of the century, Milton and Dryden. Each of these men performed certain poetic functions so magnificently well that the magnitude of the effect concealed the absence of others. The language went on and in some respects improved. . . . But while the language became more refined, the feeling became more crude.

He proceeds very carefully from here, yet is courageous enough to speculate

> . . . whether it is not a misfortune that two of the greatest masters of diction in our language, Milton and Dryden, triumph with a dazzling disregard of the soul. If we continued to produce Miltons and Drydens it might not so much matter, but as things are it is a pity that English poetry has remained so incomplete. Those who object to the 'artificiality' of Milton and Dryden sometimes tell us to 'look into our hearts and write'. But that is not looking deep enough. . . . One must look into the cerebral cortex, the nervous system, and the digestive tracts.

Half a century later, these words are grist to the undergraduate mill, yet the poet, himself at a crossroads by 1921, was speaking of a real misfortune, a tragic, and not merely noteworthy, fact of literary history that affects every writer. Turn to 'The Riddle' (p. 58):

> Drank like birds. Drew until vision would cease.
> Stars take years to reach the stomach through sighs.

The cerebral cortex, the nervous sytem, even the ever-so-unpoetic 'stomach' (in Russian, literally, 'food tract'), perceived by contemporaries as a 'Futurist' excess: they are all here. Could a Russian poet be the missing link in the evolution of sensibility whose collapse in the wake of the seventeenth century so troubled his Anglo–American contemporary?

My point here is not to prove that Pasternak is a direct descendant of Donne, Vaughan, Herbert and Marvell. There is no doubt that an indirect connection, easily documented by the minutiae of his Germanic spiritual genealogy (Shakespeare and Goethe, Swinburne and Rilke), woven into the autobiographical fabric of *Safe Conduct* and obvious in the poems, is there, however ambivalent the poet's attitude to the terminology of 'Romanticism'. The point is that we may well ask, with Eliot, 'what would have been the fate of the "metaphysical" poets had the current of poetry descended in a direct line from them, as it descended in a direct line to them? They would not, certainly, be classified as metaphysical'. So here is where these versions of Pasternak 'fit': into what might have been the mainstream of English poetry.

Eliot begins his now-famous essay with the now-famous nine lines from Donne's 'A Valediction: Of Weeping'. Turn to the poems of 'The Rupture' cycle (pp. 45–9) or 'Waving a fragrant anther . . .' (p. 25). The 'telescoping' of images, Eliot's now-famous term for the moments of 'metaphysical' revelation, seems to have been invented with Pasternak in mind.

Zanyatya filosofiyei is the name of one of the 'chapters' in *My Sister Life*. Needless to say, I render this as 'Studies in Metaphysics', not only because it describes more precisely what Pasternak studied at Marburg than the vague 'Philosophy'. In the light of everything said thus far, the risk of limiting the sense of the Russian word is justified. This, of course, is just an example of how the second Narcissus interprets his nature. The first Narcissus is always there to validate his poetic licence.

Perhaps I had better leave to others the critical exercises whereby the baroque synthesis of experience may be related to Pasternak's lyric technique. A recognition of the kinship between what was and what might have been is sufficient for my purposes. The English Pasternak must strive to possess the emotional temperature of Donne and the syntactic boldness of Milton, his uniquely Russian and uniquely contemporary qualities safeguarding the originality of the whole. But there is one aspect of this kinship which, again with Eliot's help, must be examined further.

The poems of Pasternak show at once that their author has interests: in philosophy, in music, in botany. These interests shape the poet's vast, difficult, unpredictable vocabulary, as Eliot thought they might:

> The possible interests of a poet are unlimited; the more intelligent he is the better; the more intelligent he is the more likely that he will have interests; our only condition is that he turn them into poetry, and not merely meditate on them poetically. . . . It is not a permanent necessity that poets should be interested in philosophy, or in any other subject. We can only say that it appears likely that the poets in our civilisation, as it exists at present, must be *difficult*. Our civilisation comprehends great variety and complexity. . . . The poet must become more and more comprehensive, more allusive, more indirect, in order to force, to dislocate if necessary, language into its meaning.

The English counterpart of Pasternak's Russian reader must bear this in mind. Turn to the second stanza of 'A Sultry Night' (p. 34) and a whole encyclopedia of baroque pathology seems to shed its blurry pages at our touch. 'Waving a fragrant anther . . .' (p. 25) seems to have sprung from the colour spreads of *Newcomb's Flower Guide*: 'Let the wind, *inspiring spirea*. . . .' In Russian: *po távolge véyushchiy*. Russians read John 3: 8, *Spiritus ubi vult spirat*, as *Dukh véyet, gde khóchet*, and yet it is a rare translator who has not dutifully corrected and translated these words along these lines: 'Let the wind, which blows over the meadowsweet. . . .' True, in English, John 3: 8 reads: 'The wind bloweth where it listeth.' But even if we assume, which I personally do with great difficulty, that the scriptural reference – rather than, say, Smirnitsky's *Russian–English Dictionary* – has motivated their choice, the result is not English poetry but, indeed, a verbatim quotation from *Newcomb's*, acceptable only to the spiritual heirs of Wordsworth. Thus the 'interests' of a poet are relevant only if they result in poetry.

I have written that the English Pasternak must strive to possess the emotional temperature of Donne and the syntactic boldness of Milton. Another way of saying it, as Schumann said of Chopin, is that great means are needed for great meanings. On the other hand, a contemporary critic said of Chopin's Études: 'Those who have distorted fingers may set them right by playing these.' The question here is no longer one of who is right about Pasternak, Wladimir Weidle or Marina Tsvetayeva; but rather of whether, even if one accepts the contention that there is room for Pasternak in English prosody, there exists today a critical milieu capable of treating the very idea of 'transport' with the sincerity it requires.

Of all the 'modern' poets to write in English, strangely enough, the one closest to Pasternak in temperament and attitude is Emily Dickinson, another possible 'missing link' that Eliot failed to take into account in 1921. I have published my translation of a selection of Dickinson's poems into Russian, and my love for her is second only to the one I describe here. In this connection, I propose the following experiment. Read the following lines:

> I mean to rule the earth,
>   And he the sky –
> We really know our worth,
>   The sun and I!

The experiment works only if one does not know *The Mikado* by heart, since this is sung by Yum-Yum in Act II. The talent of W. S. Gilbert is undeniable, and this excuses the confusion of many literary men whom I have convinced that the lines are Dickinson's. Indeed, when such things are taken out of context, their outlines begin to blur, and we can find Edward Lear in *King Lear* and Marshak in Pasternak.

Yet the curse of Lear, Edward, is sure to follow me as it has followed many an English poet who has had the misfortune of living in the twentieth century. Lydia Pasternak-Slater, who herself translated a few of her brother's poems into English with some success, felt compelled to point out, in a letter to *The New York Times* shortly after his death, that 'Pasternak, like Mayakovsky, the most revolutionary of Russian poets, has never in his life written a single line of unrhythmic poetry, and this is not because of a pedantic adherence to obsolete classical rules, but because an instinctive feeling for rhythm and harmony were inborn qualities of his genius, and he simply could not write differently'.

As for Pasternak's and Mayakovsky's rhyme, itself a kind of triumphal arch through which all Russian poetry inevitably progresses, there Pasternak in English passes the point of no return. Three full centuries of Eliot's 'dissociation of sensibility' weigh one down. Rhyme is no longer, to be sure, universally despised as a kind of correctional institution for the English soul; it is more like an old mine, abandoned as unprofitable long ago and now remembered only by the nostalgic townsfolk and the odd curious visitor from abroad who wants to trace his family's roots to their humble beginnings during a summer holiday. The 'progressive' critical community regards it as a sad anachronism blighting the landscape: willing as its members are to tolerate the occasional enthusiast, they are not about to welcome the conversion of this redundant enterprise into a going concern. Yet rhyme is not only the spirit of Pasternak, it is his letter.

In Russian as in English and other European languages, rhyme is above all an act of will. There is no more gross misrepresentation of the nature of rhyme than one by my fellow émigré Vladimir Nabokov who listed, in an article on his translation of Pushkin's *Eugene Onegin*, the 'six characteristics' by which 'Russian poetry is affected'. I trust that just one of these will suffice:

> 1. The number of rhymes, both masculine and feminine (i.e. single and double), is incomparably greater than in English and leads to the cult of the rare and the rich. As in French, the *consonne d'appui* is obligatory in masculine rhymes and aesthetically valued in feminine ones. This is far removed from the English rhyme, Echo's poor relation, a genteel pauper whose attempts to shine result merely in doggerel garishness. For if in Russian and French, the feminine rhyme is a glamorous lady friend, her English counterpart is either an old maid or a drunken hussy from Limerick.

This is so, of course, only if one has the ear of an accountant. Indeed, is there such a thing as 'rhyme' detached from the poet and dangling its *consonne d'appui* in no particular context? Sure enough, Nabokov is terrified that the curse of Lear, Edward, may be upon him. But what on earth is he counting? The Russian alphabet has thirty-two letters, the English twenty-six. What of it?

The assonance 'honest fingers'/'amethyst remembrance' is a rhyme in the hands of Emily Dickinson because she has faith – as do I, her reader – that the juxtaposition of these sounds mirrors the emotion which she finds herself facing:

> I woke – and chid my honest fingers,
> The Gem was gone –
> And now, an Amethyst remembrance
> Is all I own.

Would her faith have been shaken by Nabokov's grim gener-
alities about the nature of rhyme, or by the plain fact that, in
and of itself, 'fingers'/'remembrance' is not an 'acceptable'
rhyme by anyone else's standards? I shall return to Nabokov as
translator, to defend him as well as to ponder his wayward-
ness. For now, let us simply ask the question of who is more
likely to gain favour in Pieria, the 'glamorous lady', obsessed
with form in her 'cult of the rare and the rich', or the 'old
maid', writing with Dickinson's honest fingers. The faith in
the possibilities of one's language, including rhyme, is still
what Leonardo called the guide and the gate.

Here is a brief digression, with a moral. Rainer Maria Rilke
was Pasternak's Virgil, who, by his admission, led him to
poetry. Pasternak met Rilke as a child and corresponded with
him in later life. He knew German and understood Rilke better
than the authors of voluminous critical studies ever could.
And yes, he tried translating Rilke into Russian. He failed. It
does not matter why, he just did.

There once lived a man named Ludwig Lewisohn who
published, in 1946 in America, *Thirty-One Poems by Rainer
Maria Rilke, in English Versions.* He had the audacity to
announce, in his brief introduction to the 47-page book, that
poems 'cannot be split into meaning and form; they have, like
life itself, in Goethe's words, neither "shell nor kernel"'. He
went on to criticize American translators of Rilke for not
understanding this. Needless to say, the only Rilke that exists
in English to this day is Lewisohn's. Needless to say, he has
been universally forgotten, though not by me.

There once lived a man named Alexander Bisk who pub-
lished, in 1919 in Russia, his *Selections from Rainer Maria Rilke*
and reprinted his versions in Paris in 1957, not long before his
death as an obscure émigré, in a hotel fire. The book was
dedicated to his son, the distinguished French poet Alain
Bosquet, who himself had published by then a collection of
French translations of Emily Dickinson. As it happened,
Pasternak read Bisk's translations after they first appeared,

many years earlier, and wrote to Bisk to acknowledge his genius. I do not know French and cannot judge Bosquet's translations of Dickinson, but there is no doubt that the only Rilke that exists in Russian to this day is his father's. Bisk succeeded where Pasternak had failed.

In 1960 a long article in an influential émigré periodical vilified both the son and the father. Entitled 'On the Untranslatable', it savaged Bosquet for 'conveying the rhythm of the thought, not of the word' and Bisk for daring to 'compete with the author'. The verbose polyglot and tone-deaf pedant philosophizing about the 'Untranslatable' was none other than Wladimir Weidle.

Needless to say, Alexander Bisk has been universally forgotten. No, not by me. One simple, diffident truth from his introduction to the poems abides with me always:

> I translated only what enchanted me: there was no question of translating one poem after another. Any attempt to convey 'The Complete Works' of a poet, or even one complete volume of verse, is doomed to failure. . . . To translate a poem one must fall in love with it, learn to live with it, penetrate its musical essence – this is particularly important with Rilke – and only then try to say something of the kind in one's own tongue.

Bisk and Lewisohn were born translators of Rilke, translators in Tsvetayeva's sense of the word:

> Today I should like Rilke to speak – through me. In everyday language this is called translation. (How much better the Germans put it – *nachdichten*: Following in the poet's footsteps, to lay again the path he has already laid. Let *nach* mean follow, but *dichten* always has a new meaning. *Nachdichten* – laying anew a path, all traces of which are instantaneously grown over.) But 'translate' has another meaning: to translate not only *into* (into Russian, for example) but also *to* (to the opposite bank of the river). I shall translate Rilke into Russian and he, in time, will translate me to the other world.

To them, the 'Untranslatable' was something dwarfed by the 'Untranslated'. Their faith in the possibilities of their respective languages, including rhyme, overcame the resistance of the original. It triumphed over everything but the world and made them martyrs of its indifference. They too shall gain favour in Pieria.

My concern with the critical milieu is not the private obsession of a young writer. It is peculiar to the condition of a man without a country.

After 1917, the writers of Russia lost the absolute right to remind the world of their existence, forced as they were into spiritual, or geographic, exile and separated from the natural means by which reputations – 'the quintessence of all misconceptions that collect around a new name', in Rilke's phrase – are made. Deprived of that right, those too young to have won recognition before 1917 acquired it in the West only by accident, and almost always posthumously. Even in the case of Pasternak, who had acquired not mere reputation but fame – sufficient for Stalin to use him as the representative of 'Soviet' culture in the 1930s – the history of his appreciation in the West is punctuated, apart from émigré writings, by no more than two or three serious studies (notably 'The Poetry of Boris Pasternak' in the July 1944 number of Cyril Connolly's *Horizon*), until the *Zhivago* scandal made him a political celebrity second to none. Similarly, it is only when these writers were discovered to have anticipated some of the directions within the mainstream of twentieth-century literature in the West that their names began to be exhumed from oblivion: Zamyatin and Orwell, Bely and Joyce, Evreinov and Beckett, Vvedensky and Ionesco are a few obvious instances. Vladimir Nabokov is a case in point. Although saved from émigré oblivion in the mid-1950s by the scandal of 'immoral' *Lolita*, he was fair game to academic critics for decades, though not at all because *Lolita*, by the standards he had set as V. Sirin, was a commercial travesty. No, the professors of American universities criticized their Cornell confrère's command of his native tongue.

In February 1966 Nabokov published a 'Reply to My Critics' in *Encounter*. The reviews, which he summarizes, of his four-volume translation of *Onegin* are so preposterous that he swears he 'shall be accused of having invented' them. Within its own frame of reference, the 'Reply' is a polemical masterpiece, making mincemeat, in particular, of Edmund Wilson's 'pompous aplomb and peevish ignorance', and only in its last paragraphs does one get a glimpse of Nabokov besieged:

> Finally – Mr Wilson is horrified by my 'instinct to take digs at great reputations'. Well, it cannot be helped; Mr Wilson must accept my instinct, and wait for the next crash. I refuse to be guided and controlled by a communion of established views and academic traditions, as he wants me to be. What right has he to prevent me from finding mediocre and over-rated people like Balzac, Dostoyevsky, Sainte-Beuve, or Stendhal, that pet of all those who like their French plain . . . [and] why should I be forbidden to consider that Tchaikovsky's hideous and insulting libretto is not saved by a music whose cloying banalities have pursued me ever since I was a curly-haired boy in a velvet box?

Vladimir Nabokov was a Russian writer, and an American writer devoted to the study of Russian – of Russia, of Pushkin – who questioned his knowledge of Russian – of Russia, of Pushkin – committed, *ipso facto*, a critical crime. Yet the American academic community, with barely a Russian grammar between them, was openly on the side of the criminal:

> A still more luckless gentleman (in the *Los Angeles Times*) is so incensed by the pride and prejudice of my commentary that he virtually chokes on his wrath and after enticingly entitling his article 'Nabokov Fails as a Translator' has to break it off abruptly without having made one single reference to the translation itself.

Characteristically, the reviews Nabokov cites as 'sympathetic' were without exception published in Britain, where true intellectual freedom of the press has always been somewhat larger and academic communion somewhat less masonic. In America, the situation has in fact deteriorated since Nabokov's day: in 1977 the national congress of Slavists marking the thirtieth anniversary of the American Association of Slavic Studies heard 317 papers on diverse subjects, nine of which were delivered by Russian-born participants, most with misbegotten academic credentials.

No, if Vladimir Nabokov failed as a translator, it was not because he did not know Russian, or English for that matter, as well as Edmund Wilson. If Pasternak was not born to translate anyone, Nabokov at any rate was not born to translate Pushkin. The first Narcissus is but a namesake of the second.

In one of his lighter moments an American academic poet and critic, whose 'pompous aplomb and peevish ignorance' ordinarily resemble Wilson's, once compared translation, in its quotidian sense of the written equivalent of simultaneous interpretation, with a game of tennis. Translating a poem, he allowed, 'seems to be a different sort of game entirely, in which one is required to get the ball into the right box on the other side of the court, even though the area across the net may be laid out differently'. In tennis, of course, both sides of the court are identical, but that is not what makes the banal simile wrong. If we choose to enlarge that simile, we may say that the layout of 'the other side' can complicate the game without rendering it qualitatively different. It is what the game is played with, rather than on, that matters, because, however complicated the configurations of the court, the tennis-ball is certain to behave in specific ways under certain conditions known to players of certain skill. By contrast, players using a live squirrel instead of a rubber ball would be playing a game that is qualitatively, not quantitatively, different from tennis. Here is a familiar passage:

'Do you know languages? What's the French for fiddle-de-dee?'

'Fiddle-de-dee's not English,' Alice replied gravely.

'Who ever said it was?' said the Red Queen.

Alice thought she saw a way out of the difficulty, this time.

'If you'll tell me what language "fiddle-de-dee" is, I'll tell you the French for it!' she exclaimed triumphantly.

But the Red Queen drew herself up rather stiffly and said 'Queens never make bargains.'

The relationship between the quantitative and the qualitative may be likened to a general knowledge of French and the specific knowledge of what 'fiddle-de-dee' is in French. Alice may have all of Larousse in her head, but she is in a quandary all the same: she is powerless to translate the phrase because she is unable to think in the qualitative mode. Her creative impotence as a translator is what makes her assert, with the confidence of a Weidle, that 'Fiddle-de-dee's not English.' This may be harsh on the girl. But translators all over the world have had to relive Alice's consternation when they set out to visit Wonderland for themselves. As they discovered, or should have discovered, a phrase could indeed be found, say in Russian, to make the Russian Alice deny its Russianness and in so doing cover up her inability to translate it into French.

The faithful translator sees possibility in impossibility. Unfortunately the reverse is equally true. While the creative freedom offered him by 'fiddle-de-dee' is virtually unlimited, an apparently simple phrase like 'replied gravely' forces him, in fact, into a strait-jacket of anxious literalism. If nuance is what he is after, he may well begin to feel intimidated by everything easy.

The continuum of a living language is never smooth, and at any given time some parts of it are discernible more and some less, forever flowing and forming new shores of familiarity, new shoals of aloofness. Take Pushkin's *Onegin*. Nabokov, in a 1955 article in *Partisan Review*, defined his aim categorically: 'The person who desires to turn a literary masterpiece into another language, has only one duty to perform, and this is to reproduce with absolute exactitude the whole text, and nothing but the text.' Written over a century and a half ago, *Onegin* cannot be translated into another language 'with absolute exactitude' any more than 'replied gravely' can be. The language of *Onegin*, like that of the English phrase, is dissolved in language. Nabokov's standard of exactitude would require the respective contents of Murray's and Dahl's to be appended to the translation like a giant footnote. Nabokov had the good taste not to play the qualitative 'game' with *Onegin*, for he knew that the chance for that had been missed in England a century ago, when Pushkin's utterance was still a living, reverberating echo of Byron. What he did not sense was that his quantitative 'game' would not attract an English audience to Pushkin: exegesis is not a spectator sport.

Once the language of a work has dissolved in language, its translations are bound to be temporal: so, for instance, the works of the ancients are notorious for the obsolescence of their translations. In his essay 'Seven Agamemnons', R. A. Brower gives a diachronic account of Aeschylus in English:

> When a writer sets out to translate – say, the *Agamemnon* – what happens? Much, naturally, that we can never hope to analyse. But what we can see quite clearly is that he makes the poetry of the past into the poetry of his particular present. . . . The average reader of a translation in English wants to find the kind of experience which has become identified with 'poetry' in his reading of English literature. The translator who wishes to be read must in some degree satisfy this want.

Eliot, as sensitive as Nabokov ever was to the wiles of the 'paraphrasts', would have agreed: 'Greek poetry', he wrote in 'Euripides and Professor Murray' in 1920, 'will never have the slightest vitalising effect upon English poetry if it can only appear masquerading as a vulgar debasement of the eminently personal idiom of Swinburne.' The point is that, in translation, what has been dissolved in language must always masquerade. If, like Nabokov, the writer spurns the mask, the reader is justified in buying a dictionary instead of his book. If, like several other translators of Pushkin, he wears it, the reader cannot be blamed for preferring Byron.

'The gifted translator', again in Poggioli's phrase, 'is an alchemist who changes a piece of gold into another piece of gold.' To reduce a poem to its elements is plainly not enough: one must bring about their transubstantiation.

In one of the poems from 'The Rupture' cycle (pp. 45–9) the reader will come across the verb 'wed' in the imperative, conveying the Russian *posyagní!* As today's Edmund Wilsons will be quick to point out, there is little 'exactitude' here, as the word means 'infringe' or 'encroach'. I shall save them the trouble.

The ancient Russian noun *poság* means 'wedlock' and can be traced back to the Sanskrit *sajati* – he attaches. The Russian bride *posyagáyet*, grips the wedding towel and follows the groom, 'goes to marry', *idet zámuzh*. *Prisyága*, oath, is similar, since one swears by what one touches, and indeed 'stake' is one of the meanings of 'wed' in English, from Old High German *wetton*, to wager. All this of course lies beneath the surface of the word: my version imposes etymology on the reader no more than does the original. Pasternak, in a letter to Tsvetayeva, once described a lyrical poem as 'the etymology of feeling'.

Here is another example. The last two stanzas of 'For My Enemies' (p. 51), I shall no doubt be told, are especially far from 'exactitude'. Yet like the original they are steeped in Shakespeare, puzzling the discerning reader in Moscow in 1923 as they do again in London in 1989.

Perhaps I should allow Poggioli to make the point again, in what is doubtless the most gallant defence of the art by a critic:

> It may well be an error to believe that the translator has nothing to offer but an empty vessel which he fills with a liquor he could not distil by himself. One should play, at least tentatively, with the contrary hypothesis; one should even suppose, using a related, if opposite, image, that the

translator himself is a living vessel saturated with a formless fluid or sparkling spirit, which he cannot hold any longer in check; that when the spirit is about to fizzle, or the liquid to overflow, he pours it into the most suitable of all containers available to him, although he neither owns the container nor has he moulded it with his own hands. Were this true, one could even claim that translating is like pouring new wine into an old bottle; and that if the wine fails to burst the bottle, it is only because the new wine required the old bottle as the only form or frame within which it could rest.

Here Poggioli reveals his source:

To accept such a hypothesis one must believe, with the protagonist of *Doctor Zhivago*, the recent novel by the great Russian poet Boris Pasternak – who by the way is also a great translator of Shakespeare – that art is not 'an object or aspect of form, but rather a mysterious and hidden component of content'. According to such a view, the translator is a literary artist looking outside himself for the form suited to the experience he wishes to express.

In short, the 'mysterious and hidden' must never be made apparent and revealed. The poet's apocryphon is separate from his apocalypse. The translator's talent should keep him from confusing the two, and his skill heal the surgical scars left by the incisions of intuition.

Clearly the word *zhizn'* does not mean the same as the word 'life'. 'This *zh*', my father once wrote, 'is something raw, like the black sour bread in the village, burning, scalding, vital, dark, intense, and then the long *i*, in plaint and pity, bursts into the ending *izn'* like a fount, but in it the *z-z-z* is a fierce spray, like milk hitting the pail, and the palatalized *n'* is a soft nothing, the sound a baby makes when it strains to say something but knows no words.'

In 1964, when we still lived in Moscow, John Updike

stumbled upon my father's translation of Prishvin's *Nature's Diary* and later recalled its 'slightly ragged type' and 'drawings in the innocent Soviet style' as part of the English prose, 'now limpidly transparent and now almost gruff, a foxy prose glistening with alert specifics'. He was right to see it that way, for context is everything. Thus Rilke described his first moments in Moscow: 'Tired as I was, I set out, after a short rest, to see the town. . . . This spectacle, so extraordinary for me, shook me to the depths of my soul. For the first time in my life I was overcome by an indescribable emotion, as if I had found my native land.' It does not matter what Rilke had seen, the Iverskaya shrine across from the Grand Hotel where he was staying or an iridescent puddle in a cobbled street.

It does not matter what the Russian word means. In the context of an English version of a Russian poem, the English word may be *made* to 'mean' what the Russian word 'means', and sometimes more. When Pasternak uses a word, it may speak to the English reader in the context of every poem, of a whole cycle, of the entire book. It may bounce off his biography and skid through the lives of his contemporaries, whatever their language.

Philological nostalgia of the Nabokov variety is very common indeed. It is not always chauvinistic. At a symposium on translation at the University of Texas twenty years ago, Jean Paris confessed that

> The secrets of English will always defeat us. The phonetic complexity of this language, its power to reproduce thousands of natural sounds – the roaring of the waves, the howling of the wind, the dripping of the rain – make it a perfect instrument for suggestion. Compare, for instance, *profond* and 'profound': while the French adjective is purely nominative, the English one seems to possess in itself the quality it indicates: profundity is the very substance of the word, we can almost hear a voice sinking into its depths. It is this splendid music of diphthongs of which we, the French, are dreadfully deprived. . . . Thus, in English discourse, the words seem to be counterpoints, they extend in great

complexes of echoes and correspondences, which suggest
behind the logical sense an obscure world where dreams can
travel indefinitely.

What is M. Paris leading up to? 'But of course, you
Americans, you 'ave Poe.'

Yet the French Symbolists who discovered Poe were not
merely envious: they had faith in their language, and they
overtook him. However highly one thinks of Poe, the follow-
ing rebuttal by Kenneth Rexroth encourages such faith:

> Communion is as important to the poet translator as com-
> munication. I was taught the 'correct pronunciation of
> Latin', but I have never been able to take it seriously. On the
> other hand, who has ever forgotten the first time, on the
> streets of modern Rome, that he looked down at his feet and
> saw SPQR on a manhole cover? Sympathy can carry you
> very far if you have talent to go with it. Hart Crane never
> learned to speak French and at the time he wrote his triptych
> poem *Voyages* he could not read it at all. . . . Yet *Voyages* is
> by far the best transmission of Rimbaud into English that
> exists – the purest distillation of the boyish hallucinations of
> *Bateau Ivre*.
>
>   Sympathy, or at least projection, can carry you far. All
> sensible men to whom English is native are distressed at the
> French enthusiasm for M. Poe, the author of *Jamais Plus*.
> Nobody in France seems to be able to learn, ever, that his
> verse is dreadful doggerel and his ratiocinative fiction
> absurd and his aesthetics the standard lucubrations that go
> over in Young Ladies' Study Circles and on the Chaun-
> tauqua Circuit. The reason is, of course, that the French
> translate their whole culture into Poe before they even start
> to read him.

By contrast, Aldous Huxley had no time for communion
when he discussed Poe in his *Vulgarity in Literature*. People
lacking in faith are often possessed of wit, and Huxley is no
exception:

The paramour of Goethe's king rhymed perfectly with the name of his kingdom; and when Laforgue wrote of that 'roi de Thulé, Immaculé' his *rime riche* was entirely above suspicion. Poe's rich rhymes, on the contrary, are seldom above suspicion. That dank tarn of Auber is only very dubiously a fit poetical companion for the tenth month, and though Mount Yaanek is, *ex hypothesi*, a volcano, the rhyme with volcanic is, frankly, impossible. On other occasions Poe's proper names rhyme not only well enough, but actually, in the particular context, much too well. Dead D'Elormie, in 'The Bridal Ballad', is prosodically in order, because Poe had brought his ancestors over with the Conqueror (as he also imported the ancestors of that Guy de Vere who wept his tears over Lenore) for the express purpose of providing a richly musical-magical rhyme to 'bore me' and 'before me'. Dead D'Elormie is first cousin to Edward Lear's aged Uncle Arly, sitting on a heap of Barley – ludicrous; but also (unlike dear Uncle Arly) horribly vulgar, because of the too musical lusciousness of his invented name and his display, in all tragical seriousness, of an obviously faked Norman pedigree. Dead D'Elormie is a poetical disaster.

There, the curse of Lear, Edward, has done its ugly work once again. Poe's immolation in the name of his superhuman faith in the English language – or, as he called it, originality – seems 'horribly vulgar' to his jaded compatriot a century later. But martyrdom is not a refined spectacle, and the philistine always finds it vulgar. Horribly vulgar.

Apart from the critical milieu in a general sense, there exists a smaller academic community whose opinions may well inhibit the fledgling impulse of originality. Idle philosophizing is addictive, but nowhere is this addiction more conspicuous than among the 'professional' literary theorists, for whom translation is the lotus of choice.

In recent years, the internecine warfare of the lotophagi has been conducted on the sofas of Structuralism, effectively

dividing the community into two, a bad sign for the neophyte
who wishes to cling to a vision of pluralism in culture. The
radical 'Right', separated from the radical 'Left' by the
vitreous expanse of a Giacometti table, espouses a kind of
schoolmasterish fascism, most recently exhibited in an article
by Peter Jones, 'Winged Words', in the January 1988 number
of *Encounter*. Scornful of what he calls the 'social worker'
theory of literature, with its insistence on a 'structurally
correct analysis', he writes:

> If I knew what a 'structurally correct analysis' was, I should
> argue that it depends critically on faithfulness to the text. At
> least I can think of no useful purpose that could be served by
> such an analysis if it did not matter whether *arma virumque
> cano* was translated 'Arms and the man I sing' or ''Course it's
> a bleeding penalty, ref'.

The rebuttal, in the February 1989 number of *Encounter*,
came in the form of 'Who Will Translate the Translators?' by
Roy Harris, complete with obligatory references to Derrida
and Saussure. The 'Left', in literature as in politics, is always
intellectually better prepared, and it is difficult not to agree
with Harris when he identifies the argument of his opponent as
a nostalgic yearning for the halcyon days of old when the train
of thought was always on time:

> This is accompanied by a contemptuous dismissal of doubts
> on that score as due to a misguided '"social worker" theory
> of literature'. For Jones, all such attempts to undermine the
> fifth form's confidence in their Classics lessons are clearly
> subversive. 'There is nothing new to be said about trans-
> lation,' he asserts categorically. So back to your grammar
> books, Smith minor.

Should Smith minor be inclined to protest, Jones deploys
the ever powerful pedagogic strategy of ridicule. Smith
minor will be invited to stand up and say whether he
supposes that *arma virumque cano* might perhaps be rendered
as ''Course it's a bleeding penalty, ref'. The class duly

laughs, Smith minor is made to look a fool, and order is restored. Translation from the Classics can now proceed as before, soundly anchored to the certitude that chaps like Lewis and Short jolly well knew their Latin after all.

In general, it is difficult for a reader of Harris's article not to embrace his point of view without reservation: it is subtle, like being converted to communism by reading Shelley. What is seductive here is his optimism.

Poor translations are the fault of incompetent translators, not a consequence of the inherent unviability of the translational enterprise. After all, if languages *were* structurally isomorphic, then any dullard would presumably be able to translate Racine into such English verse as Alexander Pope might have envied. . . . The clever translator is someone who manages to make inadequate equipment look as if it is doing the job: an artist who specializes in verbal *trompe l'oeil* by accommodating 'what the original says' to constraints imposed by what a different language *has* to say, and by making the accommodation sound like what a gifted writer in the latter language plausibly *might* have said if expressing 'the same thought'.

Yet optimism and faith, like pessimism and truth, are clean different things, and this realization ought to keep the neophyte out of the clutches of the radicals. Their discussion, he ought to remember, remains formalist so long as neither stakes his all on an original contribution to world culture, conceived, as such contributions invariably are, in the heat of reckless idealism. The honeycombs of sandstone outside my window, with their white-on-black dactyls of *Visitors Are Not Allowed to Walk on the Grass of the College*, have grown too cold for such orgies of feeling, as Pasternak once put it.

It becomes clear that this book is addressed to poets and, by extension, to their readers: to those capable of creation or of participating in creation. It is they, not professional critics of poetry and translation, who will ultimately decide whether or not to accept the consignment I have attempted to deliver over the barriers of language and history.

My uncle, a 'distinguished' Moscow poet and 'influential' Soviet littérateur, but privately a deeply reticent man with a unique sense of humour, had an unfortunate experience early in his career. A reviewer ridiculed his Russian. 'First they criticize your Russian,' my uncle recalled, 'and then your telephone is disconnected.' To avert the escalation of official hostilities, he confronted the reviewer in the corridor of the Writers' Club and, banging the head of his nemesis against a convenient wall, whispered to him: 'Do not ever criticize my Russian.' Mysteriously, it worked.

In the West such a course of action is not advisable, if only because literary life is less centralized. Yet there are certain similarities: genuine poets, cradled by the smaller publishers, niched by the leafier suburbs, here as in Russia, are not the poets one hears most about. To them, and to their readers, this book is addressed. But what of the others, those in the public eye?

'Zhonya,' Pasternak used to confide in his sister, 'what can I do? I cannot just kill them all!' Josephine Pasternak laughs every time she tells the story. The late N. N. Vilmont, an old friend of the Pasternaks, wrote in his memoirs: 'While a man of genius is alive, it is difficult to believe in his genius. . . . The recognition is made especially difficult by the inalienable quality of genius – unevenness, even imperfection – readily discernible in the Creator of the Universe. . . . Which is why, in my own life, I find it difficult to believe in Him.' It is my aim in this book to bring Pasternak's voice to life in English for the first time. If I have succeeded, I shall also, inevitably, revive the voices of those who did not believe in his genius while he was alive. In short, I expect to hear in English ('His English is questionable . . . Pasternak does not say that . . .') what he heard in Russian ('You cannot say this in Russian. . . . He is no Blok . . .'). My failure is integral to his success.

To those in the public eye who may choose to deride this equation as the height of arrogance, I put a question: What *do* they think Pasternak should sound like? A few years ago I was asked by *The Times* to review *The Electrification of the Soviet Union* by Craig Raine, a libretto for an opera ostensibly based on the poet's life and work. I can only describe its vulgarity as shocking, and I explained why.

In 1934, all independent publishing in Russia was abolished and the Union of Soviet Writers was convened in Moscow. To add proletarian colour, workers in their work clothes welcomed their new union brethren, among whom was Boris Pasternak. As a young woman bearing a sledge-hammer walked in, Pasternak jumped up and wrested the proletarian symbol from her, thinking it was too heavy. It was, and history records with embarrassment that the poet dropped it.

By then, Pasternak had already created the verse and the prose by which Russian culture is to be measured for millennia to come and of which his later, Nobel Prize-winning *Zhivago* period is but an echo. Gentleman or male chauvinist, in his personal life Pasternak clung to the standards of his milieu. Likewise, his poetry and prose exist as a logical continuation – or culmination – of the Russian literary tradition. . . . The libretto, like Mr Raine's earlier books, stands athwart that tradition.

The Last Summer, Pasternak's vaguely autobiographical novella on which Mr Raine's libretto is based, is a miracle of poetic prose whose salient feature is its near-cryptic subtlety. For his effort, Mr Raine 'hit on the notion of an octosyllabic line' which is 'both shapely and colloquial'. Indeed, his hero tells a woman that her 'slow nipples gather closely in the cold' (he goes on to list her other enchantments), to which she replies, 'My breasts aren't bad.'

On the whole, the exchange would be jarring in a *Dreigroschenoper*. In an opera about Pasternak, it's idiotic.

Earlier I mentioned John Updike. In fairness, it should be noted that when we read his novels in Moscow we found ourselves face to face with that very same sordid vulgarity I now find in Craig Raine's representations of Russian sensibility. Updike and Raine are incidental, of course, but their artifice is a valid example of the difficulty, if not the impossibility, of glimpsing the Russian civilization into which Pasternak had been born, many decades after it ceased to exist, and relating it to the present-day civilizations, East and West, with any degree of genuineness.

The saddest heritage of the present day, and the highest barrier in the way of my transport, is emotional nihilism. Our language, in the hands of its most public users, has become so sceptical of sentiment that the simplest emotional complexity is at once perceived as affected or contrived. Since poetry is the invention of feeling, it can hardly dare to make itself public in so chilling a climate. Can anyone imagine, in these mean days, one 'published poet' writing to another 'published poet', as Tsvetayeva wrote to Pasternak in 1926, a letter beginning:

> Boris:
>   My severance from life becomes more and more irrevocable. I keep moving, have moved again, taking with me all my passion, all my treasure, not as a bloodless shade but with so green a store of food that I could feed everyone in Hades. Ah, wouldn't he give me a talking-to then, that Pluto.

No, such exchanges are now strictly private, in the sense that today these tongue-tied interlocutors are more likely to belong to that subterranean, scattered, isolated diaspora of poets and readers for which this book is intended. I can only hope that they find it, and that it finds them.

Having spoken of the difficulties, I return as promised to the essential simplicity of the translator's task. It is the transcendent simplicity of the act of creation felt by those who abscond with nature's hoard. The effortless simplicity of a miracle. What miracle? The one Pasternak wrote about in 1919, in an essay upon the truth of which, he swore to Tsvetayeva seven years later, he would 'stake his life'. It came as he was translating Swinburne in obscure, snowy Elabuga.

What is the miracle? The miracle is that once there lived a seventeen-year-old girl called Mary Stuart who sat by the window, as the Puritans jeered outside, and wrote a French verse that ended:

> Car mon pis et mon mieux
> Sont les plus déserts lieux.

It is, secondly, that once in his youth, as October fumed and feasted outside his window, the English poet Algernon Charles Swinburne finished his *Chastelard,* in which the quiet plaint of Mary's five stanzas swelled with the awesome roar of five tragic acts.

It is, thirdly, that once, about five years ago, a translator looked out of the window and wondered which was the odder thing.

Was it that the Elabuga blizzard, still troubled by the fate of the seventeen-year-old girl, spoke Scotch, or that the girl and the English bard who lamented her could both speak to him, in such clear and soulful Russian, about what still troubled them?

What can this mean, the translator asked. What is happening? Why is it so quiet out there, if the blizzard is raging? What we send forth should bleed. Instead, it smiles.

Therein the miracle. In the equality and oneness of those three, and of many others – participants and eyewitnesses of three epochs, characters, readers – before a known October of an unknown year that roars, losing its voice and sight, out there, at the foot of a mountain, in . . . well, in art.

That is the miracle.

In 1941, to the three epochs was added a fourth: Tsvetayeva hanged herself in Elabuga.

In conclusion, an autobiographical paraphrase. The paternal advice I received long before Pasternak became second nature to me was *Idealist unósit kássu* ('The idealist makes off with the cash-box'). By this advice I have lived, and by it this book has lived in me.

> Would that not imply lilacs made into garlands,
> The splendour of daisies crushed by the dew,
> Lips squandered like mad on celestial parlance?
> Would that not imply embracing the vault,
> Entwining the hands round the hero's collar,
> Would that not imply spending ages of malt
> To brew heady evenings of nightingale dolour?

Such questions were never meant to be rhetorical. To recognize this is to understand the essential simplicity of the task.

Andrei Navrozov

From *A Twin in the Clouds*

February, let ink and tears flow,
Explain February is come,
While the roaring slush below
Burns with the spring it blackens numb!

Then get a cab, in just one moment,
Through evensong and carriage clink,
Transported where the rain's omen
Looms darker still than tears and ink;

Where like pears charred to ashes,
A hundred rooks just off the tree
Appal grey sleet in sudden freshets
Of sorrow from a single stream;

Beneath them, furrows lie blackened,
Bird cries scar the silence numb,
And the more certain the less reckoned
Like sobs the lines then become.

Like brazen ashes off a brazier
Drop beetles in the drowsy garden;
Against my candle, in the azure,
The blooming worlds continue ardent.

And as if to a faith unfathomed
Into the night I am conveyed,
Where shadows of decrepit almond
Veil moonlight bounds newly made.

Where ponds are mysteries apparent,
Where apple tide blossoms high,
And the suspended orchard's derrick
Of plain wood holds up the sky.

Träumerei

I dreamt of autumn in the dim glass light,
Of friends, with you, in their motley love,
And like a falcon, tasting blood in flight,
The swooping heart alighted on your glove.

But time would grow old, and deaf, and pass,
And, lightly touching frames with webs of amber,
Dawns from the garden veined the terrace glass
With sanguine tears of September.

But time would grow old, and pass. And pliant,
Like ice, armchair silk would melt and swell,
First audible, you stumbled and grew quiet,
The dream grew silent like the echo of a bell.

And I awoke: was, like the autumn, raw
The sunrise, and the wind drew into distance,
Chasing the sled, a running rain of straw,
The running birches chasing leaden instants.

Feasts

The bitterness of rose and autumn sky,
And in it your betrayal's burning ray,
The bitterness of faces, evening light,
Wet bitterness in every line I drain.

To workshop fiends, sobriety is blind.
On rainy days we have declared war:
Four winds may be the bearers of the wine
At trysts that our future holds in store.

Heredity and death at these feasts are guests.
A quiet dawn sets tops of trees on fire,
Like bread-box mice now rustle anapests,
And rushing Cinderella changes her attire.

Floors have been swept, the table has no crumbs.
Like child kisses, verse begins to breathe.
And Cinderella hurries: carriage to the dance,
Her own two feet when everybody leaves.

Winter

My cheek is against the whorled part
Of winter, in coils like a shell.
'Places, all! We are ready to start!'
Cries, whispers and silence pell-mell.

'We play "Stormy Sea" then? That fable,
Spinning, like rope in the pail,
Where players take turns when unable?
Then – life? Then the fabulous tale

Of how sudden the end? Of death laughing,
Of crowding and clearing the way?
Then truly the sea has stopped bluffing
And the storm starts its fiery play?'

Is it the hum of the sea-shell gyre?
Is it the gossip of rooms in dead earnest?
Or, fighting with shadows, is it the fire
That rattles the door of the furnace?

So the air gusts in the vent,
Looks about, then sighs out loud,
The sound of carriages, echo, and then
The trotter is splitting a cloud . . .

As unweeded snowdrifts crawl
Right on the window frieze.
Beyond these cups of blue vitriol
Nothing has been, nor is.

From *Over the Barriers*

The Soul

O manumitted – if memory can embalm her,
O if oblivion can – committed to time,
They're holding – a soul and a palmer,
An illegible shadow – I am . . .

O when immersed even – still stone soundless,
On the tablets of verse – even when arisen,
You thrash as once did the treasonous countess,
When February came to flood the prison.

O ingrafted – appealing for your reprieve,
Cursing the times, as one does – sentries,
Like leaves, fallen years will interweave
Through the calendar garden entries.

Spring

The buds burnt to butts their unctuous essence
To lighten and lessen the burden of kindling
April. The parks grew redolent of adolescence
And forest replies redounded, dwindling.

The throat of the forest is smalted by sounds
From feathery gullets as if by a gorgon;
Then, cracking the smalt with sonatas, resounds
Some gladiator of a steel organ.

O poetry, turn into spongy Greek fossils
With suckers! Amid sticky sward then
I'd set you to rest on the slippery mosses
Of this wooden bench in this garden.

Grow yourself ruffles and frills on trees,
Swell on clouds, like a wet wafer;
And at night I shall wring you, poetry,
To benefit thirsty paper.

Swifts

The swifts of the evening are breathless with pain
Containing the coldness of sapphire.
It bursts, and subduing their breasts' throaty strain,
Comes gushing, remaining entire.

The swifts of the evening have nothing to cry of
If something up there can quench with entreaty
Their jubilant claim, exulting – O triumph,
Just look, down there, the earth is retreating!

As a pot bubbles over with fine white lace,
The quarrelsome moisture is gone;
Look there, look there! The earth has no place
From the dell to the edges of dawn.

Improvisation

I was feeding a flock of black piano keys
To the sound of splashing, of wings and of leaves.
With outstretched hands I stood on my knees;
The night grasped my elbow, clawed at the sleeve.

And there was autumn. And there was a lake
And waves. – And birds of the love breed were there,
Prepared to slay sooner than to be slain
By darkness, black hardened beaks in the air.

And there was a lake. And there was autumn.
Tar barrels of midnight were flaring and lighting
The waves that gnawed at the boat from the bottom;
And just by my elbow birds were fighting.

And darkness was stuck in the throat of the weir.
It seemed that the nestlings had tasted first blood!
Prepared to die before others could hear
From those deep gorges a throttled roulade.

From *My Sister Life*

To the Memory of the Demon

Es braust der Wald, am Himmel zieh'n
Der Sturmes Donnerflüge
Da mal' ich in die Wetter hin,
O Mädchen, deine Züge.

Nic. Lenau

He came at night
From Tamára, in the blinding blue,
Ruled with his flight
For the dream to burn and conclude.

Never wept. Never wrung, nor entwined
Bare, lashed and scarred hands.
The old stone was confined
By the fence of Georgian gardens.

As the ancient hunchback entered
On the wall tall shadows clowned like fire.
The *zurná*, by the light of the lantern,
Of the princess, barely breathing, inquired.

But the lightning raged
And contracted, the hair a phosphorous edifice.
The colossus then heard how the Caucasus aged,
Growing grey by the edge of the precipice.

Just a foot from the window-pane,
Stroking the wool of a cloak he had worn:
'Darling, sleep!' By the ice, by the rain,
'I'll return in a torrent!' he swore.

17

Sorrow

For this book's sombre epigraph
The deserts were rippling
As lions roared, and tigers' wrath
Was reaching out to Kipling.

Here the gaping empty chest
Of woe stood wide open,
And there swayed and caressed
Merino prose, hoping

For a continuous parade
Of rankless verses,
Treading the fog in shades of grey
The Ganges cleanses.

Cold mornings came next, to ease
Entwined instants
Of jungle, moist as ecstasy
Or incense.

My sister – life – is again out flooding,
Smashed, like spring rain, against what is past,
But people with pendants are subtly pedantic,
Attentively stinging, like snakes in the grass.

The elders, no doubt, have reason to wonder.
It's clear, it's clear: your wonder is small,
That lashes and lawns are empurpled with thunder
And wet mignonette spills all over the knoll.

That in May, when the timetable's diptych
Of some local line unfolds in the swarm,
Transcending the Scripture, it looks far more cryptic
Than canopies flapping off dust in a storm.

The brakes, having barked, bump the patience
Of villagers steeped in a warm rural liquor,
To watch off the mattresses for their stations
And mine as the sunset's condolences flicker.

So splashing in third, bells flow through the car
In endless regrets: I am sorry, uncertain.
And threshing the steppe from the step to the star,
The night still aglow is thrust through the curtain.

Now winking, now twinkling, now quietly sleeping!
The beloved, asleep, fairy visions unravels.
Meanwhile the heart, like a coupling, keeps leaping,
Scattering sparks through the plain in its travels.

The Weeping Garden

Horrible! – It drips and listens:
 Whether it's alone, sighing,
Lays twigs on glass and glistens,
 Or there's someone spying.

And swallowing drops, swollen
 Audibly, the porous earth yields:
Now listen how remotely fallen
 August midnight ripens in the fields.

Not a sound. It's all alone.
 Its solitude certain and utter.
At it once again – will be blown
 Over the roof, along the gutter.

Nearing my lips, become all ears:
 Whether I'm alone, sighing,
Whether I can spill the tears,
 Or there's someone spying.

Silence. And not a leaf flickers.
 Signs of vision gone. There intervene
Only gulps and splashes in slippers
 And sighs and tears in between.

The Girl

Seesaw through the garden, all ready to topple,
   A branch rushes straight at the mirror,
So huge and so near, with stray drops of opal
   Atop its nearing spear.

The garden is flustered, all scattered the islands
   Of lustre long beckoned to near,
So large and so dear, itself a great silence,
   A sister! A second mirror!

But here the branch is brought in, in a phial
   Placed by the frame of the mirror.
What is it, it wonders, that wants to beguile
   My eyes with a lay, gaol fear?

You are in the wind that marks with a green arrow
Whether it is time for the birds to sing:
Soaking, like a sparrow,
Lilac twig!

Drops have the weight of cuff-links,
The blinding garden veers
The sprinklings and the dapplings
In millions of blue tears.

The nurseling of my agonies
That you burst into thorn,
It quickens with the peony,
Exhales and forewarns.

All night it tapped away at glass
So windows had no rest
As qualms of sudden dankness
Overwhelmed her dress.

Awakened by the wondrous roll
Of names and of times,
It holds the present day in thrall
With its anemone eyes.

Rain (An Inscription)

With me at last. Then pour and laugh,
Leak through the twilight pores!
Let flow, let go the epigraph
For such a love as yours!

Go on, bob like a bombyx worm,
Molest the silk like flax!
Entangle, veil, cocoon the storm
To slant the darkness past!

No night at watch – at noon – at all!
The gravel creaks of asthma!
And whole trees are falling tall
At eyes, temples, jasmine!

Hosanna to the hosts of Isis!
Laughter is prone before the breeze!
A spectre of redemption rises
From thousands of infirmaries.

And now – we begin to list,
Like groans plucked off guitars,
Washed in the liquid linden mist,
Those garden Saint Gotthards.

In Superstition

A box with bitter-orange cells:
　　My garret.
Oh yes, I could have peeled hotels:
　　Bear it!

I move here second time round
　　Out of superstition.
The walls are papered oaken brown:
　　The door's contrition.

Never let go of the latch:
　　You tried to free.
The hair had an iris match,
　　The lips a violet spree.

O tender, for the past one's sake,
　　Free fate to will
Your dress, as snowdrops ache, to say
　　Hello to April.

To think you vestal would be stealth:
　　You entered interested,
Then took my life, as from a shelf,
　　And dusted it.

Waving a fragrant anther,
   Instilling the excellence darkling,
From blossom to blossom in transfer
   A liquid dews dizzy from sparkling.

Gliding from blossom to blossom,
   Dazzles but those, interlinking,
Twin drops, drawing agaty glosses;
   Hangs timid, flickering, clinquant.

Let the wind, inspiring spirea,
   Flatten and plumb the twin globe
Of these, entire and real,
   Kissing and drinking below.

Filled with laughter, undo the enigma
   Of bondage, to spring up full.
But drops cannot tear the ligament,
   Nor part, even if you pull.

Boating Oars

The boat is athrob in the drowsy breast,
Kissing the clavicles, willows raise
Oarlocks, elbows: please take a rest,
It really happens to everyone, always!

In the ancient songs it would even amuse . . .
Would that not imply lilacs made into garlands,
The splendour of daisies crushed by the dew,
Lips squandered like mad on celestial parlance?

Would that not imply embracing the vault,
Entwining the hands round the hero's collar,
Would that not imply spending ages of malt
To brew heady evenings of nightingale dolour!

English Lessons

And when the songs were Desdemona's,
Little was there to live for.
Not as the starry night, her leman, does:
She weeps for willows more.

And when the songs were Desdemona's,
The voice obscured her features.
Not as the rainy day, her demon, does:
The psalm of weeping reaches.

And when the songs were Ophelia's,
Little was there to live for.
With each breath the soul was kneeling as
When the wind at willows tore.

And when the songs were Ophelia's,
Her tears bittered true.
The water warned with feeling as
With columbines and rue.

And treading daffodils like passion
They entered, their trophies furled,
Into the pool of heaven, splashing
As if to deafen with the world.

A Definition of Poetry

It is a fully ripe whistle,
It is ice, shard on shard,
It is night, chilling thistle
When two nightingales sparred.

It is peas run to seed sweetly raw,
It is tears of the universe, pod–clad;
It's the stands' and the flutes' *Figaró*,
Downpouring hail on the flower–bed.

All the things that night stands upon
Like submerged bathing–boards it embalms,
And a star is transplanted into the pond
On wet trembling palms.

Flatter than planks in the water, so stuffy.
Heaven falls earthward, like an alder.
It would become these stars to be laughing,
But the universe wants a beholder.

A Definition of the Soul

Torn off like a pear come thunder,
With one leaf beyond separation.
How loyal: so willing to sunder!
Insane: into dry suffocation!

A ripe pear aslant from the storm.
How loyal: 'Not people like us!'
Turn round and look: mere form,
Burnt to ashes and fallen to dust.

Our land is all smudged by the glare.
Your nest: do you recognize it, darling?
O nestling! My leaf, are you scared?
Why keep beating, my shy silky starling!

O song grafted on to me, do not fear!
Where else on this earth can we live?
Ah, the deadliest adverb – 'here' –
Cannot quiet the spasm swathed stiff.

A Definition of Creativity

Shirt collar unbuttoned to expose its
Hairy chest, like the Beethoven torso's;
Like draughts under palm – ever posits
Dream, conscience, night and love forces.

And some piece that is barely queened,
With some frenzied sorrow in the opening –
Prepares the world for an end by the fiend,
The cavalier in a foot company.

In the garden, from vaults, ice-cold,
Stars exhale their cellared bane –
Veins athrob like the vines of Isolde,
Tristan stifles a swelling plaint.

And the gardens, the lakes, the fences,
Boiling tears to a white outpour
Of creation – so passion dispenses
What condensed in the human core.

Our Storm

The storm, a priest, has burnt a plant.
The smoke of sacrifice has veiled
Eyelids and clouds. – Rectify,
With lips, an insect's sprained eye.
The bucket clank is smashed aslant.
O why such greed: has heaven failed?
A hundred hearts beat in a ditch.
The storm has burnt the plant to pitch.

Of smalt the lea. What azure frills!
O just a touch, they are so dainty.
The smallest finch is off to find
Some pearly malt to clear the mind.
The storm, which barrel thirst instils,
Continues down from clouds of plenty.
And clovers grow brisk and brown
Under the brushes of renown.

Mosquitoes are thick as crows.
But why the siphon of malaria,
Right here, must you, devil insect,
Where summer luxuries are intact?!
Inflame the skin and strike a pose,
Red ballerina, blithe Ariel!
The goad of mischief makes a channel
Where blood is like the leaves of anil.

O trust my play, and do have trust
In migraine throbbing through the air!
Thus wrath of day is sure to spark,
A scion graft in cherry bark.
Now trustful? Now then, now thrust
Your face still nearer: in the glare
Of this your summer gone insane,
Behold its fires never wane!

I cannot hide this from view:
You hide your lips in jasmine snow,
And on my lips a snow is felt
That in my dreams can never melt.
Where shall I put a joy so new?
In verse? Into the lined flow?
Its mouth is already chapped
From poisons written pages sapped.

In alphabet it strains its sinew
To glow as a blush within you.

Sparrow Hills

Breast under the kisses as under a faucet!
Now or never is the summer's spell.
Every night some sundered doloroso
Drags along a dusty farewell.

I have heard of time: auguries are wicked!
Every ocean wave has a star to heed.
Speech is wind, and speechless is the thicket,
Heartless is the pond, and godless is the field.

Slant my soul empty! Foam it out entire!
Noontime world is here, where your eyes end.
Here thoughts ascend and catch like fire,
Scorching clouds over the pine horizon.

Here cross the rails of suburban lines.
Then there are the pines. There you cannot pass.
Then there is a Sunday. Catching at the vines,
Clearings run wild, sliding on wet grass.

Trinity and strolling through the noonday sieve:
To the groves the world is ever green.
So believes the thicket, so the fields perceive,
So the clouds spill it on the linen screen.

A Sultry Night

It fell, but had the bent restrain
The tempest in a sack of pollen,
While the dust took pills of rain,
The iron powder quietly fallen.

No blain cures saved the tuber!
The poppies swooned up to the ankles.
Rye lay embossed for want of rhubarb,
Quotidian God incised carbuncles.

In the insomniac turned sodden,
The orphaned, universal space,
Each sound had its echo trodden
By gusts of wind upon my face.

In the pursuit that followed on,
Drops ran. Then by the garden gate
The wind filled in the hollow dawn.
I held my breath. I was too late!

It seemed eternity conveyed
Those blind drops with blind force.
Unseen, I felt I could evade
The awesome garden's mad discourse.

If not, it would become eternal!
O it would carry on, infernal.

Summer

It stretched its thirsty spiracles,
Its butterflies so faithful,
Spun memories seemed miracles,
So mintful, meadful, Mayful.

The clock was still, but sound born
Of swipples, as if to sever
And pierce the air with a thorn,
Came to astound the weather.

Away sometimes, gone for hours,
The sunset put a cricket
In every bush, with powers
Over both field and thicket.

Not shadows, beams the crescent laid,
Sometimes very blatant,
And quiet, quiet nights would wade
Through moonlit clouds stately.

Rather asleep than aslope roofs, and more
Prepared to restrain than to refine,
Rain lingered, shuffling by the door,
And smelt like cork, or wine.

So smelt the dust. So smelt the breeze.
And if you want a sequel,
So smelt nobility's decrees
On who's free and equal.

While others knew the squires well,
Some knew them only partly.
Days lingered in the fields and smelt
Like cork, or wine, tartly.

What We Had

And then we had a loft of hay;
It smelt like cork, or wine.
August is gone, and since that day
Unweeded paths entwine.

The tendrils and the lips among,
Hoarse diamonds shivered, drizzling,
In their numbness to the tongue
Remíniscent of Riesling.

September was a small expense
The way we were spending:
It pruned our trees and rimed our fence,
It said the summer's ending.

Diluting wine in puddles, broke the bread
Of glaucous sand baked white,
Syringed from heaven, melting into lead
The latticed glass of light.

Or it would melt light into sand
In flight, igniting trees and eaves,
And then our glass could not withstand
The sight of burning leaves.

For there are brands of joy – the oaths
Vin gai, vin triste. Have trust –
These tendrils are but slender growths,
And Riesling – only rust.

Thus we had night. We had the strain
Of lips. Hoarse diamonds sought
The eyes, where the autumn rain
Redounded, unechoed in thought.

It seemed that we so loved to pray,
And kissed as though to miss
The briefest years that take a ray
To reach the glow of bliss.

Like music: years spent in awe,
A song would never holler –
One tremulous, uninterrupted O! –
The trembling pith of coral.

My friend, you ask me: Who will pray
For fire in speeches of a fool?

Let us free words anew,
As our garden lets – its amber rind,
Both careless and kind,
A few, a few, a few.

We must not hold our own
In so much decorous trust
Of madder and of citrus
That sprinkle the bestrewn.

Who let pine tears loose
And poured, self-effacing,
At music, at the casing,
Through the latticed sluice?

Who painted the gate
In quicken miniate,
With minium from the calix
Of trembling italics?

You ask me: Who will pray
When August grows frail,
Who lives in digression,
Who knows how to fashion

Any aspen leaf;
Since Ecclesiastes,
Masters all his grief
Chiselling alabasters?

You ask me: Who will pray
For dahlias' lips and asters',
Septembered by disasters?

For willow leaves in braille,
Leafed by caryatids pale,
Leaving an autumn trail
On the infirmary jaspers?

You ask me: Who will pray?
– Omnific god of love,
The deity of detail,
Jadwíga and Jagiéllo . . .

I do not know if the fiat
Of the beyond remains moot,
But life is rather like the quiet
Autumnal, doubtless minute.

From *Themes & Variations*

Margarita

Tearing twigs on herself like a snare of rays gone awry,
Margarita's tight clench so much more lilac lipped,
So much more hotly white than the white of her eye,
The nightingale shone, and warbled and reigned and clipped.

Exuded by grass like a smell: as quicksilver conglobes
In rains gone insane, it quivered in archil.
It astonished the bark. Out of breath, touched the lobes:
All its tongue. All atremble, continued to sparkle.

When her hand moved aslant to the eyes overwhelmed
By the glow, Margarita attracted to warbling argent
And it seemed, with the rains and branches so helmed,
An amazon, breathless, lay fallen on that forest margin.

And the back of her head with one hand is so held,
And the other is free and behind her back just to try
To unloosen that drowned in shadows helm she beheld
Tearing twigs on herself like a snare of rays gone awry.

At dusk I see you in the schoolgirl light,
A boarder. Winter. Sunlight fells the trees
Of hours in the wood where I lie in wait
For twilight's fall. Here it falls and frees.

The night, the night! A hell, a vicious oval!
Had you but known it has become communal!
It is your step, your marriage, your betrothal,
More grave than an interrogation by tribunal.

Remember life? Remember slow flakes fly,
Like doves of snow, sped abreast of silence?
The wind would quickly whirl them on the sly,
Then quickly hurl them down with such violence.

You changed places! – It placed under us
Carpets of sleds and crystal heirlooms!
For life, like blood, blew venous clouds, thunderous
With fires of flurries, pouring burning blooms!

Remember movement? Time? Merchant rows?
Do you remember tents, and crowds? You recall
The cold of copper coins – how there was
A tumult of church bells for holidays of old?

Ah, love! Alas, depiction is so scant!
What can replace you? Drops? Of bromin?
A stallion's eye, I watch the dark askant
In fear of insomnia's vast omen.

At dusk I see you pass one last examination.
I see you finish. Migraine, maths, canary.
But O at night! How thirsty, O how patient
The eyes of pills, and phials of glass, how arid!

Plait these splashes of elbows into the cold of a wave,
Palms of atlas and lust into lilies in their lithe languor!
Chant your lays, delight! Let loose! Now leash them
  for that loping play
Where forest echoes drowned the hunt in its Calydon
  clangour
And the doe Atalanta in flight from Actaeon dismayed
  at bay,
Where love was the bottomless lapis in each lavished
  neigh,
Where kisses were lapsed in as traps were leapt
  as in anger
And laughter was whole in horns carrying horses away.
– O let loose! Even looser – as they . . .

Disappointed? You thought, here's
A parting, a quiet swan's Requiem Mass?
Weighing grief, with pupils enlarging the tears
Tried on to gauge their total stress?

During such liturgies, frescos chipped off the apsis
Shaking with music, like Johann Sebastian's lip.
From this vesper forward, hatred sees lapses,
Stretches in all things. A pity, no whip.

In the dark, recovering immediately, decides
Without lingering doubts it's for the best.
That – time. That she has no use for suicides.
That even this is a snail's pace.

Just try to prevent me. Just move to extinguish
These torrents of sorrow throbbing like mercury
    in Torricelli's vacuum frame.
Preclude me, insanity – wed me, advance,
Pronounce me still! O timidity, once –
Extinguish, extinguish! Inflame!

My friend my tender O as in the flight at night from
    Bergen to the Pole
By the hot down falling off the feet of ember-geese
    like snow across the land
I swear my tender I swear it is my soul
When I implore forget and sleep my friend.

When like the corpse of the Norwegian
    ice-bound to the top
In visions of the winter that no frozen masts can move
I fuss in the auroral lights of these eyes O please stop
Calm down my friend stop crying sleep will soothe.

When just as does the North beyond the farthest homes
In secret from the arctic watchful floes
Flushing the eyes of blind seals using the midnight domes
I whisper nonsense please forget don't rub them doze.

A trembling clavier wipes off the foam.
Ready to swoon, gripping its fever,
O darling! you will say to meet my No!
In music's presence? How can we be nearer

Than chords, like pages from a journal,
Into the fire's twilight then, agreed?
O wondrous understanding, be informal,
Just nod and be astonished! You are free.

I do not keep you. Go, be good in deed.
Hasten to others. Werther has been written.
One opens windows to let the veins bleed:
These days the very air is death-ridden.

Thus they begin. When they are two,
Into the sonant dark they peer,
They warble, whistle. Words in tune
Around the age of three appear.

Thus they begin to comprehend.
And in the hum of starting engines,
As a beginning see their end,
And as a brother's home, a stranger's.

Among the roses grown wild,
This awful beauty never dies:
It cannot help stealing the child.
And thus suspicions must arise.

Thus fears ripen. Is the chasm
So deep that stars appear thinning?
When he is a Faust and a phasm?
Thus gypsies take their beginning.

Thus there open, in the quotients
Of the horizon, every time,
Like sighs sudden, distant oceans.
Thus there grows a future iamb.

Thus summer evenings can disperse
The rain in just one dream, Inspire!
Whose light their irides may curse:
Thus quarrels with the sun transpire.

Thus they begin to live in verse.

For My Enemies

O childhood, scoop of soulful wealth!
At home in any wooded region,
With roots deep in the love of self,
My inspiration and my regent!

Would tears on glass be so distinguished!
Would dried wasps and roses burn!
Would all this chaos be extinguished
To flourish like a sanguine fern!

What can be said of piano keys:
Even the chords became tribal!
Nomadic, black and phoney ease
Prepares vengeance for the libel.

A lifelike tear slanders,
Proximity to kings,
A closing door slanders,
Gay jingle of key-rings.

The grace of presents given,
The perfume of a pander,
Deceitful handshakes even,
Even magicians slander.

The smallness of the age left us,
O tender ones! And we?
O left ones – and the leftists –
Pink cheeks and ennui?

Sun! Do you hear? – Fill your purses.
Pine, are we dreaming? – Must endure.
O life, our name is – dispersal,
Unknown by sense and to your cure.

O Duncan of grey guesses! – Fate.
O hosts of legions in his omens!
O God, my Lord, what hast thou made
On our sale to the commons!

Could I forget them? My kin?
My seas? To flatter the charter?
For an orgy of feeling – into a gin?
With a storm – a partisan martyr?

To some cellar? Behind a window? In a rail-car?
To get off somewhere? Rent something, settle?
I savour this agony. Scar!
Your claws, O lioness, show your mettle.

The kindred. The seas. The ordeal
Of routine, so absurdly disciplinarian.
Don't take your revenge like this. Heal!
Oh, not you! It is I – proletarian!

It is true. I've fallen. Now don't spare!
Debased to a beast's self-impression,
I have stooped to depression:
I have stooped to despair.

We are few. Perhaps we are three,
From Donétz, from fire, from hell,
Under the grey running bark of the tree
Of clouds, of rains, of soldiers we fell
Amid councils, verses, discussions
Of art and of transport in Russia.

We have been people. Epochs we are.
Knocked down, sped past in a caravan guise,
Like tundra, to sighs of the tender car,
To the flight of the piston and ties.
We shall circle and startle and whirl,
We shall flock in a ravenous whirl –

And pass! You'll take long to abate:
Thus, striking a straw heap by morning,
Traces of wind still live the debate
Adjourned without warning
To an assembly of trees, in the hatching
Of stormy proceedings over the thatching.

Spring, I am from the street where poplars are aghast,
Where distance is appalled, the house afraid to fall,
The air is blue, like clothing bundles passed
To one discharged from hospital.

Where twilight's empty like the stark surmise
A fairy-tale star puts in a sentence
To the bewilderment of countless noisy eyes,
Homeless, and hungry for repentance.

Now shut your eyes. And in the deafest labyrinth
For thirty leagues of silent space askance,
Drip under steam the snorting and the aberrant
Cries, whispers, smiles, insomnia and trance.

Like me, they walk away when the spring barters.
That has been tried by every philistine.
In the cathedral groves, to honour these martyrs,
The engine offers cups of stolid steam.

But was it long, since in the course of service,
Led by capitulas ordained by black pine,
The worldly March filled each clandestine crevice
Along the garden paths with lilac wine?

Atonement for its sins will be my future share.
Uncorking threshing willow casks afresh,
The morning would transport the emptied tare
Into the streams in its translucent mesh.

The twilight hours would begin to harden
Both puddle pearl and river aquarelle,
With dawn as gardener to keep a guard on
First bagatelles and primer nonpareil.

In comfort, and then by banquet,
By way of *le style Jacob*,
Temperament is made languid,
A bee in a crystal globe.

Sparks scatter far and wide:
Letting your fingers roam,
You curb that demon pride
With just a simple comb.

Your pose is one of defiance
And love, and your lips a show
Of mockery, of 'Be quiet,
You are not three, you know!'

O freshness, O droplet of emerald
Teased by the wrist in motion,
O comb of chaos ephemeral,
O heaven's wondrous notion!

Autumn

Those days reached the heart of the park
With the leaves that October saw falling.
Dawns laboured at forging an end to the dark,
The elbows ached and the throat was swollen.

The fog was washed up. The clouds hit bottom.
The dusk took forever. The evening was specked,
And bared its hectic, inflamed and rotten
Horizon for busy front yards to inspect.

Then blood seemed to freeze, but that did not bind
The ponds, and it seemed to the weather apparent
That the days would not heal the unfirm hyaline,
So transparent its heaven, so pale and barren.

Then vision gained much distance, more resolute
Was eyesight, and pulse became quickened, until
A silence was spilled, and how breathlessly desolate,
How breathlessly endless rang out its still!

The Riddle

A mysterious nail left the markings:
Too late to read now, in any event.
But as I lie in the darkness
None can touch you as I did then.

How I touched you! The bronze of my lips
Touched you as tragedy touches a theatre.
The kiss was a summer. It lapsed and eclipsed,
And a storm gathered later.

Drank like birds. Drew until vision would cease.
Stars take years to reach the stomach through sighs,
While nightingales roll their eyes in ecstasy,
Draining by drop the darkling skies.

Poetry

To you, O poetry, I swear,
To you that isn't simply rain,
And not a voice one picks to wear,
But summers with a third–class fare,
But suburbs stifling a refrain,

But stuffy, like a May, environs,
A field of battle in the mist,
Where clouds moan of perseverance,
Where the horizon barks Dismiss!

Where with the rail web entwined,
As it envisions, not ensnares,
Along the lines, far behind,
Not with a song, but unawares,

Rain spouts froth and clusters frosty,
Enthralled forever by the dawn,
In eavesdrip scrawling its acrostic,
With rhyme into bubbles blown:

When, poetry, under the faucet,
Truism, like bucket zinc, lies low,
Then, even then, the stream is glossy,
Some paper underneath, and – flow!

Notes to the Poems

On 29 January 1890, in Moscow, Boris Pasternak was born into an idyll. The first child of loving parents, a painter and a pianist, he would date the beginnings of his conscious life to an evening in November 1894 when he was awakened by the sounds of Tchaikovsky's trio in A minor. His mother, assisted by two of her peers from the Moscow Conservatory, was performing the work for Tolstoy in the next room.

No member of the Pasternak family would ever pursue success for its own sake. The mother, Rosalia, a protégée of Anton Rubinstein and one of the most promising musicians of her generation, sacrificed her career to family life. The father, Leonid, is unquestionably among the most gifted painters Russia has produced, a kind of Impressionist *sui generis*, yet one who lacked the promotional skills of Diaghilev's 'World of Art' luminaries to win for himself some lasting international reputation. The children were brought up to uphold that tradition. The eldest daughter, Josephine, is a supremely talented poet, yet to this day her work remains for the most part unpublished and largely unknown.

It is for this reason that, in biographical terms, the persistent identification of Boris Pasternak with the *succès de scandale* of *Doctor Zhivago* is so contrary to the nature of the Pasternak phenomenon. In literary terms, it is even more misleading.

The year was 1912, *annus mirabilis*: Alexander Blok began the publication of his collected poems and the Silver Age of Russian culture reached its apogee. In that year the genius of young Pasternak burst in. There was no warning, no transition. At twenty-two the poet seemed to have sprung from the godhead of Lermontov. The 'biography' of one so young could not have been relevant until later, when it became the stuff of autobiography in his 1931 *Okhrannaya gramota* (Safe Conduct). Happy childhood at 21 Myasnitsky Street, an eighteenth-century town house in the heart of Moscow. Fifth Gymnasium, one of the city's best schools, which he entered at eleven. A brief encounter with Rainer Maria Rilke at a railway station in the summer of 1900, as the family was leaving Moscow to go off on a holiday in the country: 'A silhouette among bodies'. The summer of 1903 in Obolenskoye, south-west of Moscow, where the composer Alexander Scriabin, then at work on his Third Symphony, was the Pasternaks' neighbour: 'The infatuation struck.' The years 1903–1909 were accordingly devoted to the study of musical com-position, under the tutelage of Reinhold Glière, among others. The family spent 1906 in Berlin, to get away from the previous year's political turmoil at home. In 1908, admission to the Law Faculty of Moscow University – and, far more important, the discovery of a dusty copy of Rilke's *Das Stunden-Buch* in his father's library. In 1909, an impulsive decision to abandon music.

After a year at the University, philosophy was the dominant interest, and Pasternak went to Marburg to study Kant under Hermann Cohen. There, an unsuccessful courtship and the sudden realization that, as Lara put it in *Zhivago*, to study only philosophy 'is as odd as eating nothing but horse-radish' broke Professor Cohen's spell. Youth was ending. 'How infinite a thing youth is. . . . That part of our lives which is greater than the whole.' During his first post-Marburg summer the poems of *Bliznets v tuchakh* (A Twin in the Clouds) came into being:

> Thus they begin. When they are two,
> Into the sonant dark they peer,
> They warble, whistle. Words in tune
> Around the age of three appear.

Some of these were later integrated, in revised form, into the 1917 collection *Poverkh baryerov* (Over the Barriers), written in 1914–16. In 1922, *Sestra moya zhizn'* (My Sister Life), conceived in 1917, followed. In 1923 came *Temy i varyatsii* (Themes & Variations), written in 1916–22. In 1932, subsequent poems were collected in *Vtoroye rozhdeniye* (Second Birth). Together with the additions and revisions of two decades, and the four long poems – *Vysokaya bolezn'* (High Illness, 1924), *Devyatsot pyatyi god* (The Year 1905, 1926), *Leitenant Schmidt* (Lieutenant Schmidt, 1927), and *Spektorsky* (1931) – the five collections of verse written over a period of twenty years comprise the Pasternak canon in the hearts of those who understand his work and the tragedy of his life.

The first 'words in tune' appeared in print just before the First World War, when the poet's home was still the idyll it had been in his childhood. The events in the autumn of 1917 put an abrupt end to that idyll:

> Our land is all smudged by the glare.
> Your nest: do you recognize it, darling?

Shortly thereafter, the family was scattered, and the last time Boris Pasternak saw his parents was during a visit to Berlin in 1923.

The poet remained in Moscow where, despite increasingly frequent spells of despair, he continued to write and publish poems so fresh, bold and somehow immutable that by the early 1930s his verse came to occupy a place in Russian literature that bears comparison with that of Shakespeare in English.

> Let us free words anew,
> As our garden lets – its amber rind,
> Both careless and kind,
> A few, a few, a few.

Like Shakespeare, Pasternak transformed the existing poetic vocabulary, and with it the very language of Russian poetry, by the elemental force of his genius. Alexander Pushkin is often said to have 'created' the Russian literary language. If the place of the 'Russian Shakespeare' is permanently reserved for Pushkin, it can truly be said that the English equivalent of Pasternak has not yet appeared.

The spiritual world created by Pasternak between 1912 and 1932 is unique. Whether the key analytical 'section' be the sound of the poet's voice (Aseev's 'element of intonation') or the inexorable logic of his 'phantom syntax' (in Tynyanov's phrase), all attempts to dissect it end in critical failure. Significantly, Osip Mandelshtam called Pasternak 'the initiator of a new mode of prosody commensurate with the maturity and virility of the Russian language'. Marina Tsvetayeva, the poet closest to Pasternak personally and spiritually, understood this as soon as she opened a copy of *My Sister Life*. Pasternak, she concluded, was 'a poet more important than any, for most present poets *have been*, some *are*, and he alone *will be*'. Pasternak's world is lyrical. It is closed to critics, pedants and cultural paraphrasts who revel in reinterpreting spiritual realities which they are powerless to create. In this, it is more like Shakespeare than Shakespeare.

The last of the poems in *Second Birth* had been written and published in magazines in 1931. The book appeared in 1932. On 24 April of that year *Postanovleniye TsK VKP(b) o perestroike literaturno-khudozhestvennykh organizatsyi* ('Party Decree on the Restructuring of Literary and Cultural Organizations') was issued, a signal that the totalitarian state was ready to eliminate the last vestiges of independent publishing remaining from the previous decade. The myriad literary 'currents', inherited by the regime from the Silver Age of Russian culture and allowed to flow in the early 1920s, would now be dammed by decree into a single stream of 'Socialist Realism'. Officially this happened in August 1934, when the Union of Soviet Writers was convened in Moscow, but by the spring of 1932 the intention had long been clear.

By that time Pasternak's 'reputation' had been established,

and the State accepted it for what it was. What is remarkable, in fact, is the extent to which the regime's ideologues saw his work as 'constructive'. The child of a family idyll, Pasternak saw ecstasy – and not merely happiness, as the State's propagandists required – in the world around him, a world being plunged into terror and misery. Such was the nature of his joyful genius – in contrast, for instance, to Akhmatova's melancholy and Mandelshtam's wistfulness – and the State chose to interpret his ecstasy as approval of the regime. A more worldly, politically astute writer would not have been able to mistake the emerging totalitarian reality of the 1930s for an organic part of nature's universal flowing, as Pasternak had in *Second Birth*. 'In the days of the congress, six women trod fields', an immortal line in Russian from one of the poems in that collection, encapsulates the time and lives on as an example of this uniquely Pasternakian astigmatism. The regime was inclined to treat it as political vision, and the poet was duly appointed to the governing board of the new Union of Writers.

Despite the regime's benevolence, Pasternak stopped writing. In a private letter he wrote in 1953, he recalled his state of mind at the time:

> I was nineteen years younger, Mayakovsky had not yet been deified, they kept making a fuss over me and sending me on foreign trips, I could have written any filth or trash and they would have published it; I was not in fact suffering from any disease, but I was constantly unhappy and was pining away like a fairy-tale hero under the spell of an evil spirit. I wanted to write something honest and genuine in honour of the society which was so kind to me, but this would have been possible only if I had been willing to write something false. It was an insoluble problem like squaring the circle, and I was thrashing around in an uncertainty of intention which clouded every horizon and blocked every road.

To say that in time the poet's ambiguous perception of the least free political and cultural period in recorded history turned to hatred, or even fear, is to misrepresent him. 'Created before Adam', in Tsvetayeva's phrase, Pasternak was above politics, even the politics of life and death. Genius is above everything, including language.

The spiritual paralysis of the man who described himself in his odd new position as 'thrice-decorated wizard-consultant for poetry' did not, however, pass unnoticed by the regime. The ruler's displeasure was akin to the embarrassment of a host who wants to show off to his guests a prize songbird, which at that moment becomes obstinate in its silence. The suicides of Vladimir Mayakovsky, in 1930, and Tsvetayeva, in 1941, framed that silence, and there was nothing anyone could do about it, not even the poet himself.

Professionally, like many writers in the deadly stillness around him, Pasternak began looking to the art of translation for material as well as spiritual sustenance. Of the translations he was to produce during the next quarter of a century, some fifty poets from a dozen languages, Shakespeare's sonnets and plays and Goethe's *Faust* are best known. The rest was largely *khaltúra*, hack-work, as he often acknowledged. This was inevitable. Temperamentally the poet was still too full of himself, in the best sense, to bow to another's original. So even his early attempts to translate his beloved Rilke into Russian were doomed to failure.

Publicly, in his 'holy idiocy', Pasternak vacillated between curiosity, which he felt for the dictator personally, and revulsion, which he felt for his incarnation in the regime. Even in retrospect it is not clear which was the more dangerous course of behaviour: to attract Stalin's attention and insist on speaking to him 'about life and death' (as Pasternak did in the famous conversation when the dictator telephoned to ask his opinion of Mandelshtam) or to jeer openly at the sycophancy of the new 'Soviet' writers (as he did in a February 1936 speech to the Union of Writers' board meeting in Minsk). When, in 1936, mass terror reached a new height, Pasternak's actions became still more reckless, and he was duly attacked *ex cathedra* by

V. P. Stavsky, Secretary of the Union of Writers, for
'slandering the Soviet people' with a spray of pale poems about
Georgia which he had managed to squeeze out of himself that
summer. In April 1937 he refused to sign a 'collective letter'
against André Gide and, in June, one condemning Marshal
Tukhachevsky. Private indiscretions, such as his visit with
Nadezhda Mandelshtam after her husband's second arrest in
1938, continued to accumulate as well. Nevertheless, like very
few others in his circle, he survived physically. Spiritually, his
suffocation was by now total.

The disintegration of his second marriage (his first, to
Evgeniya Lurye, had broken up in 1927), to Zinaida Neigauz,
did not help matters. The war, part of which Pasternak spent
in evacuation in Chistopol, on the Kama River, was some-
thing of a welcome diversion. A new collection, *Na rannikh
poyezdakh* (On Early Trains), was published in 1943. Its poems
read as if they had been translated from the language of
Pasternak into a plodding, versified prose. A decade earlier the
revellers in *Spektorsky* drank their New Year toast to 'the
writer's becoming a poet / And the poet's becoming a demi-
god'. Now an opposite fate had befallen the poet.

As early as 1936 Pasternak began to think of prose as a way
out of his creative stupor. To be sure, he had written prose
throughout his life – but, in one critic's apt phrase, it was prose
as 'prophecy of the verse to come'. Now prose was becoming
its own prophecy.

The muse of the prose to come was Olga Ivinskaya, a junior
editor with the magazine *Novy mir*, aged thirty-four when
Pasternak, then fifty-six, met her in 1946. The 'Party Decree
on the Magazines *Zvezda* and *Leningrad*', with its denunci-
ation of Akhmatova, had just been published, as Stalin
unleashed Andrei Zhdanov on what remained of the literary
milieu in Russia. It was in this atmosphere that the
fourteen-year liaison between the poet and his muse began,
and the prose that ensued was *Doctor Zhivago*.

As Zhdanovite denunciations piled up – in March 1947 Paster-
nak was branded as 'ideologically alien' and 'full of malice' –

Olga Ivinskaya was the ageing poet's only solace, inspiration and hope. By 1948, early chapters of his novel existed in typescript, as did some of the 'Poems of Yuri Zhivago' which the novel would later incorporate. In October 1949 Ivinskaya was arrested. After several months of unsuccessful interrogation, devised to make her 'confess' by implicating her lover in a variety of political crimes, she was sentenced to five years' hard labour.

Despite his infinite grief and a heart attack he had suffered during this ordeal, Pasternak continued his work on the novel. Stalin died in March 1953, and Ivinskaya returned from the camps in the autumn. In April 1954 ten of the 'Poems of Yuri Zhivago' appeared in *Znamya*, accompanied by a note about the prose work in progress: 'The hero is Yuri Andreyevich Zhivago, a doctor, an intellectual. . . . He leaves behind some memoirs and among other papers some . . . verse, part of which is offered here and which, grouped together, will form the novel's final chapter.'

In her journal entry for 4 December 1957, Lydia Chukovskaya, Anna Akhmatova's amanuensis of many years, recorded Akhmatova's reaction to the novel, which she had just finished reading in typescript:

> There are some absolutely unprofessional pages. I suppose Olga [Ivinskaya] wrote them. Don't laugh: I am serious. As you know, I have never had editorial inclinations, but here I wanted to grab a pencil and cross out page after page. And yet the novel has landscapes . . . I would maintain they are unequalled in Russian literature. Not in Turgenev, not in Tolstoy, not in anyone.

Akhmatova's extemporaneous verdict may or may not be taken for a sober analytical assessment of *Doctor Zhivago*. Yet the fact remains that, by 1957, she was one of the few surviving remnants of the cultural milieu which had engendered Pasternak and nurtured others who in some sense could be considered his peers. For this reason, her mixed response to the novel, like her discriminating opinions about Pasternak's work before and after 1932, stands as the only reliable critical judgement by an eyewitness. As for Pasternak's own judgement, he told Chukovskaya that the novel was 'the only worthwhile thing I have ever achieved'. This corresponded with his fitful, savage, tone-deaf revisions of his early verse throughout the *Zhivago* period, which dismayed Akhmatova, and with his new, 'simple' verse, which she abhorred.

The 'Poems of Yuri Zhivago' are the last instalment of the Pasternak of *On Early Trains*, as distant from the Pasternak of *My Sister Life* as *Wellington's Victory* is from the Beethoven we know. Compare Pasternak's lines invoked at the end of my introduction to this collection (p. xxxvi) with the late poem 'In Hospital', both in translations by his sister Lydia:

> This then would mean – the ashes of lilac,
> Richness of dew-drenched and crushed camomile,
> Bartering lips for a star after twilight.
> This is – embracing the firmament; strong
> Hercules holding it, clasping still fonder.
> This then would mean – whole centuries long
> Fortunes for nightingales' singing to squander.

And the first seven lines of the other:

> They stood, almost blocking the pavement,
> As though at a window display;
> The stretcher was pushed in position,
> The ambulance started away.
> Past porches and pavements and people
> It plunged with its powerful light
> Through streets in nocturnal confusion . . .

'Deep into the blackness of night', reads the following line. The banality is unstoppable, mechanical. The 'meaning' is clear. The poet is dead.

Thankfully, in his prose the contrast was less pronounced. As a novel, despite the fundamental weaknesses quickly glimpsed by Akhmatova, *Zhivago* endures, condensing all that had remained of the supreme genius of Russian poetry in his later years into a prose style. Certainly against the backdrop of the cultural wasteland which was Stalin's Russia, this was a remarkable achievement.

The prospects for its publication, whether in a journal like *Novy mir* or by the State publishing house in book form, being quite dim, in May 1956, against the entreaties of both his wife and his mistress, Pasternak, ensconced in his country house in Peredelkino, fifteen miles from Moscow, passed on the type-script of the novel to the Milan publisher Giangiacomo Feltrinelli. Soon thereafter tentative arrangements for its serialized publication collapsed altogether, and – despite persistent attempts by Soviet literary officials to dissuade him – Feltrinelli published the novel in November 1957. The émigré of a novel, the first on record since writers like Pilnyak and Zamyatin were pilloried for publishing abroad some thirty years earlier, became a best-seller and a *succès de scandale*. On 23 October 1958 its author was awarded the Nobel Prize for Literature.

According to Ivinskaya, his love unto the last, the *Zhivago* scandal 'broke and finally killed him'. Pasternak developed lung cancer and died in hospital on 30 May 1960. He was buried in Peredelkino, where his novel was written.

A Twin in the Clouds

It is not in keeping with my views of Pasternak's life and work to cite his own views expressed after the years of silence during which his voice left him for ever – that is, after the publication of his prose autobiography, *Safe Conduct*, in 1931, and of his fifth book of verse, *Second Birth*, in 1932. Yet poets rarely speak of their earliest years until they have completed the process of autobiography by means of which their imaginary career is made. The retroactive action of *Safe Conduct* does not uncover, and often, with a capriciously shifting focus, occludes, the quotidian of circumstances under which

Pasternak's first poems came into being, because the book, like all of Pasternak's writing before 1933, lives for its own pleasure and feels no obligation to relate anything. The direct speech of art is figurative and intransmutable. It is only about Pasternak over the age of forty-three that one can ask, as he was asked by his Marburg professor about Kant, 'Was meint der Alte?' This is what the old man meant at sixty-seven, as he recalled the youth of twenty-three summering in the village of Molodi, where he came with his family in distant 1913 after his last term at Moscow University.

At the bottom of the park a small stream wound its way in whirling pools. Over one of these deep eddies, a large old birch tree broke and continued to grow upturned. The green confusion of its branches created an airborne gazebo over-hanging the water. In their sturdy weave one could sit and even recline. This I made my study. In the thick of the tree, during two or three summer months, I wrote the poems of my first book. The book, with pretentiousness bordering on foolishness, was entitled *A Twin in the Clouds*, in homage to the cosmological sophistries for which the titles of books by Symbolists and the names of their publishing ventures were known. To write these poems, to scratch out and restore what had been crossed out, was a profound need and a source of incomparable and verging on tears pleasure.

I tried to avoid romantic excess, impersonal captivation. I had no intention of thundering from the stage to make white-collar employees recoil from these poems, outraged: 'How degenerate! How barbarous!' I had no wish for flies to die from their modest elegance, or for lady professors to say, after hearing them read to a circle of six or seven admirers: 'Allow me to shake your honest hand!' I did not strive for the rhythmic clarity of song or dance which, nearly indifferent to words, quickens hands and feet. I did not relate, reflect, represent, or react to anything. Later, for the sake of unnecessary comparisons between me and Mayakovsky, oratorial and intonational beginnings were diagnosed in me as well. This is wrong. I have them no more than any man speaking. Quite to the contrary, my abiding concern was with the content, and my abiding hope was for the poem to contain something of value, a new thought or a new image: for it to be etched, in all its singularity, deep into the book, where it would speak from the pages with all its silence and all the red letters of its black and colourless typeface.

All of this may help us to understand why Pasternak has not left a definitive name by which to call his poems written before 1914. These earliest poems were collected in *A Twin in the Clouds*, his first published volume, produced in an edition of two hundred by The Lyric, an association of young writers, in January of that year. Only a few of the poems from the book were retained, revised and made part of the final canon which he arranged in 1928. In the 1929 edition of *Over the Barriers* they were grouped under a descriptive heading, 'The Early Years', but I have chosen to emphasize their provenance.

The reasons for this may not be apparent at this juncture, but they exist all the same. What is clear is that one must draw a line between other people's opinion of Pasternak and one's own, and this is as good a place to start as any: 'You play Bach your way,' Wanda Landowska was once quoted as quipping, 'I shall play him his way.' That Pasternak, unlike Bach, did not die shortly after completing his *Art of the Fugue*, complicates matters, but it does not change the essential truth of Landowska's individualism, or love under another, less boastful name.

'February . . .': First published 1913. Line 5: The vehicle in question is of course horse-drawn, a hansom.

'Like brazen ashes . . .': First published 1913. Line 1: Not necessarily, but possibly, a brazier used to fumigate fruit trees.

'*Träumerei*': First published 1914. The Russian word meaning both 'sleep' and 'dream' is here replaced with the title made famous by Schumann.

'Feasts': First published 1914. Line 5: The original has

'offspring', but the negative sense of 'spawn' is amplified by the well-established word combination, outside of which it is rarely used, meaning 'fiend'. 'Workshop', as in English, is both an artist's studio and a craftsman's workroom.

'Winter': First published 1914. Line 5: 'Stormy Sea' is a parlour game. Line 27: Cups of vitriol used to be placed between window-frames to prevent condensation. Vitriol, a white powder, absorbs moisture and turns blue.

Over the Barriers

Over the Barriers, originally subtitled 'Second Volume of Verse', was first published in 1917, carrying an epigraph from Swinburne:

> To the soul in my soul that rejoices
> For the song that is over my song.

As with *A Twin in the Clouds*, many of the fifty-odd poems in the book underwent extensive revision, but in the end most became part of the 1928 canon. 'With the passing of years,' Pasternak recalled in 1946, 'the notion of "Over the Barriers" evolved in me. From the title of a book it grew into the name of a period or a manner, and under this heading I would join together things written later, so long as they matched that first book in character.'

Earlier, in *Safe Conduct*, Pasternak tells how he was startled into the manner, and over the barriers, by the spectre of a spiritual dead end he saw in Mayakovsky:

Had I been younger, I would have quitted literature. But age interfered. After all the metamorphoses, I did not dare to redefine myself for the fourth time.

Something else happened. Time and a mutualism of influences bound me to Mayakovsky. We had some coincidences in common. I noticed them. I realized that unless I did something with myself, they would become more frequent. I had to protect him from their commonness. Not knowing how to put it, I decided to break with its cause. I broke with the romantic manner. Thus arose the unromantic poetics of *Over the Barriers*.

But beneath the romantic manner, henceforth proscribed, lay a whole world-view. This was the understanding of life as the life of a poet. It came to us from the Symbolists, and the Symbolists had absorbed it from the Romantics, especially the Germans.

This world-view possessed Blok only for a time. In the form that was natural to him, it could never have satisfied him. He either had to intensify it or leave it. He chose to let this world-view go. It was intensified by Mayakovsky and Esenin.

In its symbolism, that is in all that shares a conceptual border with Christianity and Orphism, in the poet who offers himself as a measure of life and pays for it with his own life, the romantic vision is compellingly bright and incontrovertible. In this sense something eternal is embodied in Mayakovsky's life and, deaf to epithet, Esenin's destiny, bound on immolation as it begs to be ushered and entering in the fairy-tale.

But without the legend this romantic plan is false. The poet at its foundation is inconceivable in the absence of non-poets, who place him in relief, because this poet is not a living person absorbed in moral study but a visual-biographic emblem, which needs a background to provide it with visible contours. Unlike passion plays which must have a heaven to hear them, this drama must have the evil of mediocrity to be seen, as romanticism must always have philistinism, for with the loss of conformity it loses a good half of its content.

The understanding of biography as a spectacle was a thing of my time. I shared that concept with everyone. I parted with it while it was still undemandingly soft for the Symbolists and neither invited heroism nor smelled like blood. First of all, I freed myself from it unconsciously, breaking the romantic devices that held it up. Secondly, I eschewed it consciously as unsuitable glamour, because having limited myself to the craft, I now feared any poeticization that would put me in a false and inappropriate position.

'The Soul': First published 1917. The original title in *Over the Barriers* was 'The Ingrafted One'. Line 7: The treasonous countess named in the poem is Countess Tarakanova, imprisoned in the Peter and Paul Fortress and drowned when it was flooded in 1775.

'Spring': First published 1917. The original title, deleted when the poem was grouped with two others under the title 'Spring' in the 1928 revision, was 'Poetry in Spring'. Line 5: Smalt, here and elsewhere in my versions, is enamel. But here also, as in Dante's *Inferno*, IX: 51: 'Vegna Medusa: sì 'l farem di smalto', when the three furies wish for Medusa to come and turn him to stone.

'Swifts': First published 1917. Swifts rarely alight, and even gather their nesting materials on the wing.

'Improvisation': First published 1915. The title was clarified in 1948: 'An Improvisation for the Piano'. I introduce that clarification in the first line (which has merely 'a flock of keys' in the original).

My Sister Life

My Sister Life was published in Moscow in 1922 and in Berlin the following year. Unlike the poems of *A Twin in the Clouds* and *Over the Barriers*, the poems of this book were not revised and became part of the 1928 canon as first collected. The epigraph from Lenau's 'Das Bild', appropriated here by my version of 'To the Memory of the Demon', appeared on a separate page, following the dedication, 'Dedicated to Lermontov', printed on the title-page beneath the title *My Sister Life* and the subtitle 'Summer 1917'.

In Berlin in 1922 Marina Tsvetayeva recorded her first impressions with these words: 'Before me is Pasternak's book *My Sister Life*.' When the review appeared, it brought the two

poets together, and Tsvetayeva did not conceal that she was
writing it 'from sheer cupidity: it is a precious thing to become
part of such a destiny'. Pasternak, she wrote, 'does not yet
know our words; his speech seems to come from a desert
island, from childhood, from the Garden of Eden; it does not
quite make sense, and it topples you. At three this is common
and is called "child". At twenty-three it is uncommon and is
called "poet". (Oh, equality, equality! How many did God
have to rob, even to the seventh generation, to create one
Pasternak like this!)'.

Pasternak was of course a decade older than in Tsvetayeva's
example. But she was thinking back on 1912, when his first
poems were written, and she was right. When she herself was a
decade older, in 1933, she developed that instinctive revelation
into a coherent vision of Pasternak under the title 'Poets With
and Without History'. There she wrote: 'Boris Pasternak is a
poet without development. He began with himself in the
beginning and this never changed.' Before her was the first
edition of Pasternak's Collected Poems of 1933: '1912–1932.
Twenty years. Half a thousand pages.' Every one of those
twenty years, in short, was a year of My Sister Life, as a
mountain range may bear the name of one of its highest peaks.

'To the Memory of the Demon': First published 1922. The
poem was itself something of an epigraph. It opened the book,
prefacing its ten cycles: 'Whether It Is Time for the Birds to
Sing', 'The Book of the Steppe', 'Diversions of the Beloved',
'Studies in Metaphysics', 'Song Epistles, so She Would Not
Be Sad', 'Romanovka', 'Attempts to Separate the Soul', 'The
Return', 'To Helen' and 'Afterword', the last nine parts of this
decameron originally called 'The Book of the Steppe'. I apply
the epigraph from Lenau to this first poem because I do not
wish to delete it altogether, as I do the cycle headings, nor do I
want it to overshadow what is, after all, only a selection from
the book. 'The Demon' is a poem by Lermontov: a banished
angel soars over the Caucasus and appears to Tamára, a
Georgian princess, in her dreams. Line 6: 'hands' is implicit,
not explicit, in the original, and 'arms' is suggested in Blok's

'Demon' of 1910, but a subject is more necessary here than elsewhere and this one is more pianistic. Line 11: *zurná* is a Caucasian musical instrument akin to the flute, the word itself being of Persian origin (from *sûr*, 'joy', and *nâj*, 'reed').

'Sorrow': First published 1922. Line 1: The book here is probably 'The Book of the Steppe', although in the volume's simplified, post-1928 arrangement the line would refer to *My Sister Life* as a whole.

'My sister – life . . .': First published 1922. The dash between the second and third words of the first line of the poem, and in late variants of the title of the book, is a revisionist scar. It appeared in later editions, and I follow suit, with mixed feelings, hoping that the English language will finally heal the wound. Line 10: 'some local line', in the original, is the Kamyshin branch of the Tsaritsyn railway. Line 17: 'in third', in a third-class compartment. Line 22: The original contains a reference, deleted here, to Fata Morgana, an apparition sometimes seen in the Strait of Messina.

'The Weeping Garden': First published 1922. The slippers undoubtedly belong to the poet, walking up the terrace steps to return inside.

'The Girl': First published 1922. I have deleted a two-line epigraph from Lermontov, as did Pasternak for the 1933 *Collected Poems*. Line 2: The mirror envisioned here is a pier-glass, whose three sections reflect the blossoming branch set before it and the garden beyond.

'You are in the wind . . .': First published 1922. Pasternak tried to identify the metaphysical addressee of the poem in 1945 by supplying it with a title, 'Dawn'. Line 16: 'her' is not in the original, but the 'dress' in this line, in modern Russian usage, is a woman's dress.

'Rain (An Inscription)': First published 1922. The full title is 'Rain: An Inscription on The Book of the Steppe', this being the second cycle of poems, and initially a unifying name for most of the cycles, in *My Sister Life*. It is to 'The Book of the

Steppe', recently completed, that the poem is addressed. As the only poem from this cycle of seven for which I offer a finished version is 'In Superstition', the title is abridged here. Line 5: Bombyx is a genus of moths which includes the silkworm moth. Line 20: 'Saint Gotthards' here, by extension, are the chasms in rain-drenched foliage, listed and mapped like Swiss mountain passes.

'In Superstition': First published 1922. Line 1: The Russian word for the fruit of wild, or bitter, orange used in the original is a borrowing from the German, *Pomeranze*. A picture of the fruit adorned matchboxes popular at the time. In the winter of 1913–14 and again the following autumn Pasternak rented a tiny room in Swan Passage in Moscow.

'Waving a fragrant anther . . .': First published 1920. The poem was entitled 'The Kiss' at the time of its first publication. Line 9: spirea is a common flowering plant, often spelt spiraea, belonging to the family *Rosaceae*. It has dense clusters of small pink or white flowers, like meadowsweet.

'Boating Oars': First published 1918. Line 10: The hero, named in the original, is Heracles (Hercules).

'English Lessons': First published 1922. Line 1: Pasternak fractures the traditional Russian stress of 'Desdemóna' with his English 'Desdémona', adding a stress mark to make this clear here and again in the next stanza.

'A Definition of Poetry': First published 1922. Line 6: Pasternak's 'pod-clad' is a dialectal usage, easily misunderstood as a word meaning 'shoulder-blades', which the poet felt compelled to clarify in a footnote. Line 7: Mozart's *Figaro*, here and in the original, is stressed as indicated by the accent on the last syllable.

'A Definition of the Soul': First published 1922. In the Russian the first stanza, in contrast to the other three, rhymes AABB in the original. In my version, it conforms to the ABAB pattern of the poem.

'A Definition of Creativity': First published 1922. Line 2: It is hardly of any importance that in none of the images of Beethoven we know, such as the paintings by Mähler (1815), Schiman (1818), or Stiler (1820), can his chest be seen. The important thing is his hair. Every contemporary observer felt obliged to remark on what, unbeknown to him, amounted to a visual emblem of Romanticism. 'A truthful eye beamed from under his bushy eyebrows,' Louis Spohr recorded. 'The reception room in which he greeted me', wrote Johann Tomaschek, 'was as disordered as his hair.' 'His hair, which neither comb nor scissors seem to have visited for years, overshadows his broad brow in a quantity and confusion to which only the snakes round a Gorgon's head offer a parallel,' Sir John Russell remembered in *A Tour of Germany* (Edinburgh, 1828). Line 5: In a game of draughts or checkers, a piece that makes it all the way across the board is queened, like a pawn in chess. The term used by Pasternak is obscure, and he added a footnote explaining it. Line 8: Here the scene shifts to the chess-board, with the Devil as a mounted knight among pawns.

'Our Storm': First published 1919. In the first edition of *My Sister Life* this poem was followed by an explanatory note, later deleted: 'These diversions came to an end when she passed her mission on to a substitute.' The next poem in the cycle is entitled 'The Substitute', beginning 'I live with your photograph.' Here, as with nearly all of my versions, I have retained Pasternak's rhyme scheme, although visually the original is divided into ten four-line stanzas and one couplet. Line 1: The plant named in the poem is Pasternak's beloved lilac. Line 22: As Pasternak has it, the mosquito, stinging through the blouse, poses like a 'red ballerina' – that is, a Soviet dancer on a foreign tour, an allusion much too vague for the English reader. Line 24: Anil is a shrub from whose leaves and stalks indigo is made. Line 27: 'wrath of day' – that is, Judgement Day – *Dies Irae*, and by association the Latin hymn included in the Requiem Mass.

'Sparrow Hills': First published 1922. Sparrow Hills, an elevation just outside Moscow which was not unlike old rural Montmartre, has been asphalted over and is now called Lenin Hills. Line 1: I am compelled to use 'faucet' instead of, for instance, 'tap'. Pasternak has something else in mind, thinking instead of a type of metal wash-stand for outdoor use, a savage contraption best rendered by the word used here. It finds its way into my collection once more, albeit for slightly different reasons, in the penultimate line of 'Poetry' (p. 59). Line 15: The Sunday in question may or may not be Trinity, the Sunday following Whit Sunday, in the last stanza.

'A Sultry Night': First published 1922. Line 1: 'It' is the rain, manipulating the reeds. Line 5: The stanza caused a great deal of critical consternation, compelling Pasternak to add a foot-note to at least one line and to introduce a bland variant in 1945, replacing the name of an infectious disease, absent here, with 'fever'. My version is true to the original variants. Line 21: The 'it' here refers to the 'discourse' of the garden, which in turn becomes the subject of the final line.

'Summer': First published 1922. The last two stanzas evoke the Great Reforms of the 1860s and 1870s, which created the *zemstvo* as part of a system of local government. The initial mandate, revised in the year of Pasternak's birth, required that 42 per cent of the *zemstvo* deputies came from the gentry and 39 per cent from the peasantry, the rest being merchants, clergymen and the like.

'What We Had': First published 1922. The link to the previous poem justifies its insertion here, although in *My Sister Life* it falls into the subsequent cycle, 'Afterword', coming after the next poem. Line 8: The unorthodox stress, especially in a line containing a proper name and a foreign word, is true Pasternak, like his 'uneducated' stresses in Russian words so natural to Moscow speech. Line 22: *Vin gai, vin triste* would be footnoted by a Russian editor ('Wine of gladness, wine of sadness').

'Let us free words . . .': First published 1922. The epigraph is from another poem in *My Sister Life* for which I do not have a finished version. Here is the concluding stanza of 'Balashov' (a town in the Saratov province), whence it comes:

> My friend, you ask me: Who will pray
> For fire in speeches of a fool?
> By rule of linden, rule of rail,
> By fire summer was to rule.

Line 7: Madder is a herbaceous plant of the genus *Rubia*, especially *Rubia tinctorum*, from which a crimson dye is made. Line 14: Quicken is a name for the rowan-tree, which bears clusters of red berries in autumn, and minium is a name for the red oxide of lead which has given us the word 'miniature'. Line 31: 'the infirmary jaspers', stone floors in hospitals. Line 35: Jadwiga and Jagiello are the Polish queen and the Lithuanian prince whose betrothal united their nations in 1386. The Jagiello dynasty ruled until the sixteenth century.

Themes & Variations

This is a minutes younger twin of *My Sister Life*, a parallel development of words from the same seed: published in January 1923, directly after the Moscow edition of the earlier book and almost simultaneously with the Berlin edition, it contained everything written between 1916 and 1922 that did not fit the overall scheme of Pasternak's lyrical decameron. Like the poems of *My Sister Life*, the poems of *Themes & Variations* became part of the 1928 canon without revisions. Pasternak insisted on using the antiquated spelling *varyatsii* in preference to the modern *variatsii*, and the ampersand in my version of the title pays homage to that quaint singularity.

'Margarita': First published 1920. Pasternak's relationship with Goethe's *Faust*, which he translated into Russian late in his life, may well be a subject of special study. This poem was

initially part of a 'Faust' cycle. Margarita is not of course a
spelling of the name of Goethe's heroine common in English,
but I prefer it to plain Margaret. Line 6: Archil is a kind of
lichen.

'At dusk I see you . . .': First published 1922. Line 22:
bromin, a variant pronunciation and spelling of bromine, is
by popular misconception the substance (actually potassium
bromide) prescribed as a sedative.

'Plait these splashes . . .': First published 1922. This and the
subsequent four poems are part of a nine-poem cycle entitled
'The Rupture', that is, the lovers' final quarrel, a break-up.
The five versions here (Pasternak's numbers 4, 5, 6, 7 and 9)
are presented in a slightly different sequence to capture the
variation of tone. Line 5: The hunter Actaeon surprised
Artemis bathing and the amazon Atalanta was outrun by
Milanion, but accounts of the myths vary.

'Disappointed? . . .': First published 1922. Line 6: J. S. Bach
(merely 'Sebastian' in the original).

'Just try to prevent me . . .': First published 1922. Line 2:
Evangelista Torricelli, Italian physicist and secretary to
Galileo, concieved a design for the barometer.

'My friend my tender O . . .': First published 1922. Line 5:
The Norwegian is Amundsen and, by extension, his ship. In
1918 Amundsen made headlines when he turned to air ex-
ploration (hence the 'flight' in the opening line).

'A trembling clavier . . .': First published 1922. Line 10:
Goethe's *The Sorrows of Young Werther* and, by extension, the
novel's hero.

'Thus they begin . . .': First published 1923. This and the
subsequent three poems are from a five-poem cycle entitled 'I
Could Forget Them', here in a different sequence.

'For My Enemies': First published 1923. The title in the
original names the enemy as slander, here made more general
and 'classical', as in the Russian.

'Could I forget them? . . .': First published 1923. Line 2: Charter in the sense of a train booking. Line 3: Gin in the sense of an instrument of torture.

'We are few . . .': First published 1923. The original manuscript title of the poem was 'The Poets', although it is untitled in *Themes & Variations*, where it first appeared. A presentation copy of the book was inscribed by Pasternak to Tsvetayeva with the words 'To the incomparable poet Marina Tsvetayeva, "from Donetz, from fire, from hell".' Tsvetayeva, for Pasternak, was one of the poets of whom there were 'perhaps only three'.

'Spring, I am from the street . . .': First published 1922. This and the subsequent poem are from a group of five entitled 'Spring'.

'Now shut your eyes . . .': First published 1923. Line 6: 'philistine' should be pronounced, as the rhyme requires, with a long 'i'.

'In comfort . . .': First published 1923. In *Themes & Variations* this preceded the 'Spring' poems and is here out of sequence. In the book it follows the opening poem of the book's final cycle, 'The Unquiet Garden', of which all the poems that follow here are also part. Line 2: Pasternak is more specific: 'By furniture in the Jacob style'. The firms of Georges Jacob and his son François Jacob-Desmalter, Jacob Frères and Jacob Desmalter & Cie, were the leading makers of furniture of all forms in the Empire style, both before and after the Revolution, until the Jacob tradition ended with the sale of the family business in 1847.

'Autumn': First published 1922. This poem opened a group of five entitled 'Autumn', in which the following poem came last.

'The Riddle': First published 1923. This poem, untitled in the original, ends *Themes & Variations*.

'Poetry': First published 1922. This poem is out of sequence. Line 7: The battle alluded to in the original is Borodino.